028.7

PETERLEE
COLLEGE LIBRARY

014-10

Penguin Books
Finding Facts

D1471787

This book is due for return on or before the last date shown below.

13 do
07

19. OCT 2000

Don Gresswell Ltd., London, N.21   Cat. No. 1207   DG 02242/71

FINDING FACTS FAST

Alden Todd and Cari Loder

628.7
PETERLEE
COLLEGE LIBRARY
W14-10

PENGUIN BOOKS

PENGUIN BOOKS

Published by the Penguin Group
Penguin Books Ltd, 27 Wrights Lane, London W8 5TZ, England
Viking Penguin, a division of Penguin Books USA Inc.,
375 Hudson Street, New York, New York 10014, USA
Penguin Books Australia Ltd, Ringwood, Victoria, Australia
Penguin Books Canada Ltd, 2801 John Street, Markham, Ontario, Canada L3R 1B4
Penguin Books (NZ) Ltd, 182–190 Wairau Road, Auckland 10, New Zealand

Penguin Books Ltd, Registered Offices: Harmondsworth, Middlesex, England

First published 1990
10 9 8 7 6 5 4 3 2 1

Copyright © Alden Todd and Cari Loder, 1990
All rights reserved
The moral right of the authors has been asserted

Filmset in Monophoto Melior
Printed in England by Clays Ltd, St Ives plc

Except in the United States of America, this book is sold subject
to the condition that it shall not, by way of trade or otherwise, be lent,
re-sold, hired out, or otherwise circulated without the publisher's
prior consent in any form of binding or cover other than that in which
it is published and without a similar condition including this condition
being imposed on the subsequent purchaser

ID No: 9t000474

Dewey No: 028.7

Date Acq:

Contents

A Word to the Reader 1

I *About This Book and Research in General*

Your Approach to Research 3
You Have to Practise 4
Mixing the Skills of Four Specialists 5
First Think Through Your Research Plan 8
Five Ways to Find Out 9
Six Classes of Written Material 13
For Computers Go Elsewhere 14
Be Realistic about Purpose, Time and Cost 15

II *Levels of Research*

BASIC APPROACHES 17

Finding the Right Library 17
Finding Special Libraries in Your City 19
Dealing with Librarians 20
The Best Guide to Reference Books 21
Finding Reference Books in Libraries 22
Index to *The Times* 23
British Humanities Index 24
Periodical Indexes: the Two Levels 25
Help at the Bookshop 31
A Low-Cost Home Reference Collection 32
Getting Library Discards for Yourself 34

Biographical Research: Basic Steps 34
No Reference Source is Complete – or Perfect 38
Professional Tips on Note-Taking 39
Public Relations Sources 42
The 'At-the-Binders' Gap 44

INTERMEDIATE TECHNIQUES 44

Access to Library Stacks 45
Know the Reference Book Catalogues 47
Indexes to Newspapers Other Than *The Times* 48
Biographical Reference: A Few Useful Books 49
Finding Periodicals on Particular Subjects 51
Is There a Directory That Can Help? 53
Associations – Key to Finding Specialists 54
Government as an Information Source 55
Looking In on Parliament with Hansard 56
Her Majesty's Stationery Office 58
Citizens Advice Bureaux Are Ready to Help 60
Information Networks at Your Service 61
Research Gold in the Filing Cabinets 64
Finding the Person Who Knows 68
Requests for Information That Get Results 70
Interviewing 72

ADVANCED TECHNIQUES 74

Search out the Trade Press 75
The Librarians' Guide to Reference Books 77
Interlibrary Loan 77
Finding Unpublished Doctoral Dissertations 79
Digging into Manuscripts and Papers 81
Publishing an Author's Query 83
Obtaining Out-of-Print Books 84
Oral History Collections 86
Specialized Sources of Information 87
Library Classification Systems Can Help You 89

Services from Periodicals 89
Beyond the Written Word: Multimedia Sources 90
Keeping Alert to New Technology 91

References 94
Index 98

A Word to the Reader

Finding Facts Fast is for everyone – for all who do research in business, the professions, volunteer committees and politics. It is for students at all levels who need to find out something and do not know where to look.

This is a practical and sometimes irreverent book. You can learn from it how to find out what you want to know, with speed and accuracy. You can learn to avoid the time-wasting needle-in-haystack methods by which most people search for information.

The heart of this book is the skill of problem-solving and the approaches to fact-finding that it offers. We do not propose to ask the reader to become a walking encyclopaedia of memorized sources of information, even though many such sources are to be found here. With practice any diligent person can master the research methods appropriate to his or her immediate purpose or line of work, without memorizing things that he can look up easily.

The British edition of *Finding Facts Fast* is the result of the combined experience of the authors. Alden Todd, the author of the original American edition, contributes the experience of nine years of research in the Library of Congress, where he wrote books and magazine articles for a living. While there, he was challenged by the richness of the collections around him to learn how best to exploit them. He began to question reference librarians, scholars and (outside the Library) other professional writers, seeking the most efficient research methods. Today he still keeps on with this search. One result of Alden Todd's inquiry was a course in Research Techniques and Fact-Finding, which he taught at New York University. This book is the other.

Cari Loder brings to this book the experience of conducting research in many areas of higher education and teaching a postgraduate course on research methods and study skills at the University of London, Institute of Education. Much of her research work has involved producing comprehensive bibliographies on obscure subjects within very tight time restrictions. This combination of theory and practice has led her to develop an informed, highly realistic and effective approach to research at all levels. Cari Loder is currently Research Officer at the Centre for Higher Education Studies at the Institute of Education.

C.P.J.L. & A.T.

I About This Book, and Research in General

Your Approach to Research

As in learning anything worth while, you should proceed at your own pace in learning research techniques. It does not matter whether you start in school, in college, as a research degree student, or in business, professional or public life when you are years away from formal education. Take these pages step by step, with self-confidence but without careless over-confidence.

Examine the reference sources mentioned here; you will be surprised at what you find out about the way in which reference books are organized or indexed, and at what they contain. New editions of reference sources you have used before may contain additional information or features that make them more useful than they used to be.

Don't think you can remember everything; take notes on new information and put them where you can find them later.

- Be specific rather than general in inquiries and note-taking, or you may find that you must do the job again
- Never hesitate to ask for information; the person who knows is usually glad to tell you, and respects you for wanting to learn

- Cultivate persistence in research; the most common failure is to give up too soon

- Above all, enjoy the adventure of searching in order to find out; achieving knowledge can be intensely satisfying.

You Have to Practise

Right from the start, face the fact that reading this book, even studying it, is necessary but not sufficient. To become a good researcher you have to practise. The reader should study the methods of research described in this book, then put into practice the techniques it suggests.

Gaining ability in research is rather like learning to cook well. Excellent cooks are not required to memorize five hundred recipes unless they want to. But after a bit of practice they learn how to use a dozen or more spices, when to sift the flour, how to control oven temperature, and where in the cookbooks to look up their favourite recipes.

It is the same with the techniques of research. You need enough practise to learn how to get quickly on to the trail of what you want to find out, and how to follow it to the end without being diverted. Practice in research work need not be lengthy or painful. But a certain amount of practice is essential to give you the 'feel' of how to go about it, and the self-confidence to improvise new methods. Then absorbing new and more sophisticated techniques becomes easier. Practice develops your ability to make the right moves from the start. Practice is what separates the 'pros' from the amateurs.

The first-year student who learns and applies the 'Basic Approaches' section of this book (pp. 17–44) will have become a more skilled researcher than most graduates are today. The methods described here can be an aid to much better performance, and higher grades – particularly in writing papers in English, History and the Social Sciences.

Unfortunately, lecturers often pay too little attention to showing undergraduates how to find information, in the campus library and elsewhere.

Mixing the Skills of Four Specialists

A first-class researcher needs techniques that combine the skills used by four kinds of professionals: the reference librarian, the university scholar, the investigative reporter and the detective. There is no reason for you to learn everything that these four specialists should know in order to do their jobs well but the excellent researcher should learn certain essential skills used by each, and combine them so that they support one another. If you learn well, you come out with a broader and more generally useful range of abilities than any single one of these specialists commands. It is by combining these abilities that you can become a skilled specialist in research.

The techniques described in this book are therefore a mixture of source references, methods, tips and warnings that have been taken from the training of the librarian, the scholar, the reporter and the detective. We do not pretend that they are the ultimate methods, or the final word on the subject, because new techniques and resources are constantly emerging. What is new in this book, we believe, is the systematic mix of practical techniques taken from the scholarly, professional and business worlds and presented in a clear, logical form. We believe there is something new here for everyone, including the old 'pros'.

A word now about the strong points, and weaknesses, of the four types of professional whose special abilities contribute to this mix of research techniques.

The Reference Librarian
Trained in a College of Librarianship, reference librarians

can be a masterful source of information on printed sources – especially reference books. They are usually as strong and as broad in their knowledge, as the reference collection with which they work. This may mean an entire library, or only part of a library. The average reference librarian, although an expert in their speciality, may know relatively little about sources outside their own collection, and may be almost totally unaware of research techniques other than those appropriate to the reference library.

The University Scholar
University scholars may be the most learned specialists within a limited field, and may be acquainted with every important book, manuscript collection, expert and other source which has a bearing on their speciality. From them you can learn techniques that emphasize thoroughness. Their research produces new information, or brings to light facts that previously had been buried in written accounts lost in the darkness of libraries and archives.

For most people, to try to imitate the level of thoroughness of the academic researcher is both unrealistic and inappropriate. Most of us are operating in a world that makes fresh demands on us each day. We can admire the patience and thoroughness of the university scholar and yet remember the value of our time.

The Investigative Reporter
Investigative reporters are frequently excellent all-round researchers, because the nature of their work has taught them to combine speed with thoroughness. Their strength lies in their ability to interview the person or persons who witnessed an event, and to put an account of it in writing for the first time. Good reporters know how to find their sources, how to ask the right questions, how to interpret responses, and where to find experts who can help them

put today's event into the right context – and to do all this under the pressure of a publication deadline. A good reporter who turns from daily newspaper reporting to writing a magazine article or a book, will study background material from the library as the scholar does, though usually not so voluminously or in such depth.

The principal difference in method between the news reporter and the scholar is that the reporter's priority is to complete the research in order to produce the written account, whereas the scholar often emphasizes the research process itself, with thoroughness as the goal, rather than merely publication for payment. For researchers, the art lies in combining the strong points of both. The reporter who has learned thoroughness of inquiry from the scholar can become an outstanding journalist, and prestigious awards are won by such writers. The scholar who knows when to stop digging and to start shaping what he or she has found for presentation, and who is a skilled communicator, can become the author of best-selling books.

The Detective
Detectives are frequently not far behind the investigative reporter in their all-round ability to find out what they want to know – but they usually work within the limits of their world of law enforcement. Their great asset as researchers is their familiarity with human behaviour patterns within their field. This enables them to cut through a confusion of details much more rapidly than the average person, and determine the handful of most probable places in which to search for answers. They are familiar with official documents, municipal archives, confidential indexes, credit ratings of individuals, and the like. Their experience has taught them to reason out the most likely places in which to search for what they want to know. More than anyone else, the fictional detective Sherlock

Holmes taught the world the value of thinking a research problem through first – and then looking in the places that offer the greatest promise.

First Think Through Your Research Plan

As the authors have found to their cost, it is only after wasting considerable time in research for your own professional writing that you recognize the importance of thinking through a research project, and planning its general lines before digging in. Beginners often make the mistake of rushing to the first possible source of information that occurs to them, when they should take a few minutes to consider several possible sources, then choose carefully the best order in which to follow them. In some cases it may be important to decide exactly what it is you want to find out, how far back in the literature you are going to look, what your subject boundaries are. In other words, set yourself reasonable limits within which to work. This will be particularly important when compiling bibliographies or conducting literature searches – but it will not always apply to all fields of inquiry.

In research in history, biography and events of the recent past, particularly when you are looking for printed material, you can frequently get results if you play detective and ask yourself the following questions:

> Who would know?
> Who would care?
> Who would care enough to have put it in print?

By following this procedure, the researcher might quickly come up with conclusions like these in specific cases:

> What was the sterling value of the property loss in a recent big fire or storm? Because insurance companies

paid the property loss claims, they cared enough to compile their loss records. And because several companies must have been involved, the total loss figure is likely to have been compiled by the trade association of insurance companies.

Another case:

Where should I look for biographical material on a distinguished British architect who died a few years ago? First, in the obituary pages of the national newspapers such as *The Times*. Second, in the pages of the periodical or journal of the special group of which he was a member – in this case the Royal Institute of British Architects.

The pages that follow abound in specifics on where to look for what kind of information. For the moment, our purpose is merely to stress the importance of stopping to think through your plan of research. Five minutes may be enough, but pausing to think may save a wasted hour or day – or longer!

Five Ways to Find Out

Research is not all paperwork, or reading. There are five basic ways to find out what we need to know, and **reading** is but one of them. The others, as we classify them, are:

- **Interviewing**, or asking other people, both orally and in correspondence

- **Observing** for yourself

- **Reasoning** what must be the fact from what you have learned by other means

- **Empirically researching** in order to obtain evidence to support an idea of your own.

In some research projects, using only one or two of these methods is sufficient to reach your desired end. However, it is always worth while to remain alert to all five methods, in order to make sure that you have not overlooked a fruitful source or an important part of the story. Consider the five methods briefly:

Reading
Most of what people want to know has already been put on paper – somewhere, sometime. The difficulty for most of us lies in our not having the means, or the knowledge, to find the right books, articles, manuscripts and other written materials. We do not have universal subject indexes and in many parts of the country it is difficult to obtain some written materials that we know about. A large part of this book is devoted to showing how to search for written materials and to get your hands on them.

Interviewing the expert or source-person
When facts we want have not been put in writing, at least not to our knowledge, we can try to find the people who know and ask them. (For example: the survivors of a disaster of years ago which has not been fully documented; or intimates of a political figure, now dead, who can discuss the behind-the-scenes actions of their late friend or relative.) The interviewer's written account of such source-people's stories may then become the first documentation on the subject.

Interviewing and reading are closely connected, and they complement each other. Reading can lead the researcher to the source-person who can fill in the gaps in the written record. Those we interview can often point us towards written sources that we have not yet used. (Biographers, for example, who track down surviving relatives or friends of their subject often discover valuable documents that have long lain untouched and unknown in attic and cellar.) For the academic researcher, tracking down an expert who can suggest the most important written works on the subject in question can often save long hours spent in a library trying to find relevant books.

Observing for ourselves

When we want to know what has not been put satisfactorily in writing, and when we cannot find anyone who can tell us, we must sometimes use our other faculties to gather information. This is the method of research basic to the natural sciences and to exploration, such as the space flights of the astronauts, or Captain Scott's trek over the Antarctic ice to the South Pole, or Captain Cook's voyages to the Pacific Ocean. In searching for history books, biographies and even for fiction, writers often find it useful to immerse themselves in their locale in order to gather information of an atmospheric nature – how things look, feel, sound and smell. Such direct observation is interwoven with reading and interviewing.

Reasoning from what we have learned

Concluding what must have happened, or what must be the case now, from facts we have learned by other means is the most elusive and taxing method of fact-finding. It is heavily employed by archaeologists and geologists, whose science rests on reasoned conclusions from evidence in the earth. It is the method most misused by historians and biographers: the many so-called 'lives' of William Shakespeare, the playwright/poet, rest shakily on the skimpiest of documentation, and are pasted together with presumptive terms such as 'probably', 'can be assumed to', 'perhaps', 'is supposed to', and the like.

Reasoning from the known to the unknown in research is best used as a method that leads to new documents and sources, and therefore to finding out more than standard bibliographies and other sources have provided. It is a method that should be used from the beginning in drawing up a research plan, in order that the most likely sources are covered before those that are merely possible sources.

Empirical research

Carrying out empirical research is rather like **reasoning** from what we have learned and **observing** for ourselves but differs in one important way. Empirical research is most often undertaken by graduate students studying for research degrees at universities. The essence of this method is that the researcher will be looking for evidence to support some theory or idea that he or she has, and that has not been researched by anyone else before. This method will, by definition, make use of all the others:

- **Reading** in order to find out if the subject has been researched before.

- **Interviewing** in order to obtain information from various people. For example: a psychology student who may be interested in the connection between study methods and success in university examinations would interview students in order to find out how they study and then compare this information with the examination results.

- **Observing** the situation/person in which we are interested can provide us with different information from that gained by interviewing the person. 'What people say they do is not always the same as what they actually do.' In empirical research it is important to be clear in our own mind exactly what we are trying to discover – it is very easy to be side-tracked by superfluous information. This method is in some ways a 'last resort' inasmuch as most of the other methods will have been exhausted first.

Six Classes of Written Material

Too often research time is wasted in hunting for the written materials we need, when it might be spent productively in using them. Therefore, an important element in research skill lies in getting your hands on the right material *fast*.

Reading material can be divided into six general classes because the methods for locating materials in each differ, and so are best explained separately. These classes are:

- Published books

- Magazines and journals (learned society periodicals)

- Newspapers

- Special duplicated documents that are not published (that is, not generally and freely circulated) and not copyrighted, such as: reports of organizations intended for internal or restricted use; rosters or organization members; calendars of organization activities; newsletters of small organizations, etc.

- Manuscripts (or 'papers'), meaning unpublished and unduplicated documents, such as letters, notes and diaries. These are generally handwritten or typewritten. Most historians and librarians use the terms manuscripts and papers interchangeably

- Unpublished theses and dissertations. These are manuscripts written by students and submitted to fulfil either all or part of requirements for a Master's or doctoral degree. These manuscripts, although not normally published, will usually be lodged in the college or university library at which the student studied.

Strictly for convenience in organizing this book we have classified various specialized written sources under the six headings above; for example, newsletters fall under the magazines heading. The reader can locate them in the Index.

For Computers Go Elsewhere

The authors have decided not to include in this book a thorough explanation of the use of computerized databases, even though they are useful time-savers. This book is devoted to basic principles which good researchers should be able to absorb whether or not they have access to a data retrieval system. General comments on recent technological developments in the storage, retrieval and transmission of information can be found starting on p. 91, but a detailed discussion of the use of the computer in research is beyond the scope of this book.

There are several reasons for this. First, a discussion of the various services offered by many organizations would be out of date in a short time as new programs, services and companies enter the information industry. Second, for most of the fact-finding tasks in our daily lives, we do not need nor can we use a computer, as the following pages show. Third, the information transmitted to the researcher by computer is the result of research first done by someone before the data reaches the computer stage. That work is no more thorough or accurate than the person compiling the data. So the researcher who trusts the output from a computer is really trusting the accuracy and diligence of the person who compiled it. The authors believe it is better to learn the fundamentals of doing research for oneself, and only then make use of computerized databases with due caution.

For those who wish to explore the use of computerized services in their own field of inquiry, professional librarians and other specialists can provide both practical advice and suggest literature to read.

Be Realistic about Purpose, Time and Cost

The right way to go about a research project can vary according to the time, money and manpower available, and the purpose of your search. To write a weekly paper for an undergraduate university course, a student can afford only so much time. For this purpose it does not make sense to travel to a distant city in order to consult books in a major library for a half day. But for a doctoral thesis a serious graduate student will cross the country to study the rare books and the manuscripts which the task requires. For a definitive book or magazine article, a skilled and conscientious writer will go to great lengths to gather fresh data. A hack writer, on the other hand, will crank out books and articles simply by reading and reorganizing what more conscientious researchers have written from original sources. This is the case because the hack writing market does not pay enough to permit more thorough and careful work.

The desired end result, or purpose, should bear some sensible relation to the time and money spent in research. A busy professional in the £15,000 a year class should spend ten pounds without hesitation for taking photocopies that will save a day's work, whereas a 21-year-old student might well choose to save the money. Or if a few pounds' worth of long distance telephone calls will speed up a committee chairman's work by several days, the money is well spent.

Unless the purpose of a research project is to exhaust every conceivable resource in a given search, you can set your own commonsense limits. In presenting the more sophisticated research techniques contained in the 'Advanced Techniques' section (pp. 74–93) we trust that users of this book will remember that the name of the game is not search, but *find out*. If the last 10 per cent of your planned research time has brought excellent results, you are doubtless on a productive new track and should extend the project. But if the last 25 per cent of your scheduled time has brought greatly diminished results, this fact may be a signal to wind up your research. It all depends, however, on your having established a productive plan for your research project at the outset.

II Levels of Research

BASIC APPROACHES

The methods, techniques and approaches discussed in this section are those considered by the authors to be absolutely essential for anyone engaging in research. Some readers may find that there are techniques or sources of information mentioned in later chapters that are essential to them right from the beginning, depending on what the nature of their research is. For instance, if you are a student taking a Master's degree in education you may find that you need access to unpublished theses very early on in your work – whereas a biographer may never need to. Therefore, be prepared to look through the contents pages to see if there are more advanced techniques that you would profit from mastering now.

Finding the Right Library

'Just go to the library and look it up,' is what students are frequently told. Easily said, but not always so easily done. The library may be of no help if it does not have what you need, or if you cannot easily find what you need in it.

Most people live within easy reach of a number of libraries – more than they know – and some of these libraries can serve their needs much better than others. It is useful to learn what each of the following types of library in your area has to offer:

- the public libraries of the borough, city or county

- the university, polytechnic and college libraries

- the special libraries, so called because they are devoted to collections on limited subjects, and are usually run by private organizations such as corporations, social agencies, museums or professional societies. Most people know little or nothing about the thousands of special libraries, and special subject collections within general libraries, literally dozens of which may be in their own part of the country.

A first step in surveying the local library resources is to ask an experienced professional librarian (**not** just anyone behind a desk in a library). The head librarian and others on the staff with professional training as librarians are usually members of the Library Association, and through it have contact with their professional colleagues in the same area. In the course of their work they must frequently refer readers to other nearby libraries, or arrange with neighbouring libraries for the interlibrary loan of books, so they are likely to know one another.

A second step is to consult the **Aslib Directory of Information Sources in the United Kingdom**, which reference librarians are likely to keep behind the library main desk for their own frequent use. This is the standard directory listing all sorts of libraries and sources of information in the UK. First published in 1928, it is now in its fifth edition, issued in 1982, with a sixth edition in preparation. The *Aslib Directory* consists of two volumes. Volume One, with about 3,300 entries, is devoted to science, technology and commerce; Volume Two, with about 4,100 entries, includes sources of information in the social sciences, medicine and the humanities. Entries give the name of each information source, whether a library or an organization with its own special collection of materials; address, telephone and telex; a brief description of the organization or library; the person to whom to direct inquiries; the subjects covered in the collection; special information services offered (such as computer connections); special collections within the general framework described above; and publications.

In choosing which library to use, remember that the total size of the library is less important to you than the strength of its collection in the subject field in which you are interested. Usually the special library will have a more thorough collection of materials (books, periodicals, manuscripts, illustrations and maps) in its particular field than will any but the greatest general library. In addition to the depth of its collections, the special library offers other advantages to the researcher. First, its experienced staff members will usually have a more detailed knowledge of the materials under their care than one can expect from the reference librarians in a general library who are not specialists. Second, the special library staff are likely to have more time to serve the needs of a reader because they have much less reader traffic to deal with. Third, the special library is likely to be quieter, and may offer easier access to facilities, such as duplicating equipment.

Some who would like to use a private special library (such as a corporate or law firm library) are afraid that they would not be permitted to use it because, in principle, it is not open to the public. In a very few cases this may be so, but usually the librarian in charge of a special private library will extend the courtesy of its use to an outsider who gives evidence of having a bona fide intent.

Finding Special Libraries in Your City

One of the most valuable research aids that you can acquire

is a list or directory of the special libraries in your own geographic area. This is especially true of large cities such as London where the special library resources are so great. Most librarians at your local library will be able to tell you if there are any special libraries or collections in your area. However, the best way to find out is to consult the *Aslib Directory* (see p. 18). This will provide you with information about all special collections on your subject – not just those in your local area. There are other alternative sources that will provide information about the location of special libraries and collections. These include: *Library and Information Networks in the United Kingdom*, the *Libraries, Museums and Art Galleries Year Book* and pamphlets which are published for each region by the Library Association Reference Special and Information Section, known as Library Resources for that region.

Dealing with Librarians

Professional librarians are normally graduates of a college of librarianship and will have been through a rigorous training leading to a Bachelor's or Master's degree. In the course of their training they will have been exposed to a wide range of reference materials, and should be able to guide readers to them.

It is well worth the trouble for the serious researcher to cultivate the acquaintance of librarians in a position to help. Librarians serve so many people who never say 'thank you' that they welcome a library user who speaks to them by name and shows appreciation for their knowledge and help. A librarian will often look up material in response to a telephone query – saving the researcher a trip – if the researcher has shown appreciation. Also a librarian who takes a personal interest in your project may over a period of time bring to your attention a number of source materials that you have overlooked. In this way, the librarian-friend can be a highly useful and skilled research ally.

Take the time to search out a really first-class reference librarian to whom you can turn confidently for help. Unfortunately, libraries sometimes employ people who will say, 'We don't have it,' when they really do not know, or who will dismiss your research queries with only minimum effort to help. Write these off as a lost cause and try elsewhere. The librarians to seek out are those who take every request for help as a challenge to see if they and the library's resources can meet your research needs.

The Best Guide to Reference Books

Of all the lists of reference books available, possibly the most useful and best edited is **Walford's Guide to Reference Material** published by the Library Association (see p. 77). For American literature **Reference Books: A Brief Guide** (published by Enoch Pratt Free Library) is highly recommended. By keeping these books to hand and becoming familiar with them, students and researchers can save time by first determining which reference books appear most useful to their inquiry, then telephoning to find out which of them are available at local libraries. Because so many reference books are so well described in these source booklets, readers are strongly urged to make themselves familiar with the contents. A reference copy can normally be examined at the local library. It would be wasteful to duplicate in these pages the descriptions of many reference books, and tips on how to use them which are contained in these guides. It is much better to spend your time getting to know the contents of the guide and develop the habit of using it regularly.

Finding Reference Books in Libraries

It is well worth the time to ask a librarian (or more than one) whether there is a standard reference book that covers the field in which you are seeking information. At the start, random searching through the open reference shelves wastes more time than it is worth. You can consult the library card catalogue to find out whether the library has a certain book whose title you know, but usually the librarians are familiar with their most frequently used reference books and can tell you where they are shelved. Because some of these books have considerable commercial value, they are frequently kept behind the circulation desk to be handed out only on request.

The best place to start is to consult the library's own catalogue. All libraries will have some sort of catalogue system which lists all material by author, subject or title. After consulting the library's own catalogue, it is most effective to start by asking a librarian for help in general terms. Go to the specific, or detailed, later. The reason for this is that a typical librarian is more likely to know the category in which a book is classified than to know the details it contains. Therefore, it would usually be more productive to start by asking for a standard reference book on higher education, rather than to ask where you can find out who is the Vice-Chancellor of Lancaster University. Once you have been shown the *Education Yearbook*, you can find your own answer – or ask for further help.

Good results are often obtained by approaching librarians with a question phrased something like this: 'What standard reference books do you have in the field of (general)? What I am trying to find out is (specific).'

An especially good librarian may suggest more than one title, all of them useful, or perhaps go further and bring in a book that pinpoints the object of a reader's research. But this is a matter of luck – rarely encountered in a general library, though much more often in a special or university library. As you become more experienced in research, you become familiar with the specific reference books and other sources that you have found useful and can go directly to them.

Index to The Times

The most valuable of British newspaper indexes to the researcher is the index to *The Times*. The official index has been published since 1906, and was preceded from 1790 to 1941 by *Palmer's Index to the Times*. The *Index* is now published monthly, with annual cumulations. Since 1973 it has included references to the *Sunday Times*, *The Times Literary Supplement*, *The Times Educational Supplement* and *The Times Higher Education Supplement*. The *Index* can be found in most major libraries in the UK.

The New York Times Index, bound in annual volumes, contains brief abstracts of the contents of that newspaper, arranged chronologically under subject headings, with date, page and column references. It is the best quick American source of information on events of the past several decades because: its coverage of events has been so extensive since it became a great newspaper early in the twentieth century; the indexing is so thorough; and it is relatively easily found in British libraries (such as the Colindale).

The primary value of using the indexes to *The Times* (both American and British) early in a research project is to find out the exact date of an event, to check proper names, and to get the gist of what the paper printed about it at the time and subsequently. Then the research trail can lead in several directions, such as:

- to the back copies of the paper itself, whether in bound volumes or on microfiche, to read the articles for which the Index gives date, page and column

- to the back copies of other newspapers, especially those published in the city where the event occurred, in which coverage is likely to be more thorough than that in *The Times*

- to other periodicals, such as magazines, learned-society journals and newsletters, likely to have referred to the event.

British Humanities Index

The *British Humanities Index*, issued quarterly by the Library Association, is the best single source from which to find references to recent and past periodical articles, which the researcher can then read in libraries. It is widely available in public and college libraries both in the UK and abroad. The *British Humanities Index* helps one find the answers to three kinds of question:

- What articles on a given subject were published in periodicals of general circulation in a specific period?

- What articles by a certain writer were published in that time?

- Exactly where (which periodical and issue) can one find an article where one has a partial reference, but not a full citation?

The *British Humanities Index* lists the articles published in more than 300 British periodicals of general circulation, but not those printed in many specialized journals in science, medicine and other technical disciplines. It

includes significant articles from certain national newspapers, such as the *Guardian*, the *Observer*, *The Times*
and the *Sunday Times*. It does not include those from
British editions of such widely circulated magazines of
American origin as *Good Housekeeping*, *Time* and *Reader's
Digest*. The researcher can examine the list of periodicals
covered by the index to determine which are included and
which are omitted from coverage.

The index is issued quarterly as a subject index only. At
the end of the year the four quarterly issues are cumulated
into an annual bound volume, with both subject and author
entries. Each entry gives the title of the article, author(s),
periodical title, volume number (date and year), pagination,
illustrations, portraits, and sometimes further references.

The *British Humanities Index* was first issued under
that title in 1962. It superseded the *Subject Index to
Periodicals*, which had been published since 1915, with the
exception of the years 1923–5. Its American counterpart,
which has indexed articles in periodicals of general circulation since 1900, is the **Readers' Guide to Periodical Literature**.

Periodical Indexes: The Two Levels

For comprehensive research in periodical articles the **British Humanities Index** is insufficient, because it is largely
concerned with magazines and newspapers of general circulation and covers relatively few specialized periodicals. In
thorough research it is important to consult periodicals at
both levels – the general and the specialized. To find
articles in the latter, one should consult one or more other
indexes covering specialized magazines and journals in a
broad field. Listed in the following pages are several such
indexes carried in general reference libraries and in special
libraries that divide among them the main areas of human

concern with relatively few gaps. There is some overlapping in the periodicals they cover. One should take care to read the introduction describing how each index is to be used and what its limitations are, because they are issued by different publishers and so are organized differently. As can be learned from the introduction to each index, some include references to newspaper articles and books as well as magazine articles, and some contain brief abstracts, or summaries, of the articles listed. Most include in their coverage significant publications issued in the USA and other countries.

Antiques and Collector's Index:

This quarterly index is based on comprehensive coverage of about twenty periodicals devoted to antiques and various kinds of collecting hobbies, plus other articles in this subject-field assembled from the editors' scanning of more than a hundred additional periodicals. Books dealing with antiques and collecting are also included. The *Antiques and Collector's Index* is published by Clover Publications.

British Education Index (BEI):

BEI is published quarterly with an annual cumulative volume and covers over 200 British and international periodicals of permanent educational interest. The information provided for an article includes the title, the author(s), the number of pages, the issue's number, or date, and the title of the periodical in which it was published. The *Index* is presented in two sections: the 'Author List' in which the user can check if a particular author has published an article or track down an article if only the author is known, and the 'Subject List of Articles' in which articles are arranged by subject headings. The researcher should bear in mind that although *BEI* provides comprehensive coverage of British material (excluding editorials, news items and reviews) it covers little or no American material. The *British Education Index* is published by the University of Leeds, Brotherton Library, Leeds. For true international coverage the research should also refer to the *Current Index to Journals in Education* (see below).

Clover Information Index

Nearly a hundred periodicals in the hobby, recreation, popular science and travel fields are covered in the *Clover Information Index*, which is issued quarterly. The emphasis is on magazines of practical information, including those on electronics and computers. Entries are arranged alphabetically by subject. The *Clover Information Index* is published by Clover Publications.

Current Index to Journals in Education (CIJE)

CIJE is published monthly by the Oryx Press, USA, with semi-annual cumulative issues in March and September of each year. *CIJE* covers articles published in over 780 major educational and education-related journals that are published throughout the world. The *Index* is divided into two main parts; the main entry section and the 'Subject Index'. The main entry section contains complete information about every article included in the current issue. The most useful feature of *CIJE* is that it provides an abstract for each entry. This allows researchers to decide whether the articles will be of use to them without having to go to the trouble of reading the article itself. The 'Subject Index' lists articles under subject headings and gives the reader a reference (the EJ or accession number) to the main entry section. Each monthly issue also contains an 'Author Index', a 'Journal Contents Index' and a complete 'Source Journal Index'.

Current Technology Index:

The *Current Technology Index* covers more than 300 British

periodicals in all branches of engineering and chemical technology, including the various manufacturing processes based on them. It is issued monthly, and is cumulated annually in a bound volume. It replaces the **British Technology Index**, which was published by the Library Association from 1962 to 1980. The *Current Technology Index* is published by Library Association Publishing Ltd.

Indexes to Legal Periodicals
Because all sorts of issues of human concern are continually the subject of litigation and of court rulings, articles in the law journals discussing them can be most useful to a wide range of researchers – not merely lawyers. However, subject indexes that assist one in finding such articles are not widely known outside the legal fraternity. In fact, the researcher may have to gain admission to a specialized law library in order to find them, as well as copies of the journals to which the indexes refer. Three indexes can be most helpful:

Current Law Index, a monthly published in California by Information Access Company, with periodic cumulations. It indexes more than 700 law periodicals in the UK, the US and other countries.

Current Law, a monthly publication consisting largely of abstracts of the most recent rulings in Britain, but also with citations of the latest articles on the same subjects that have appeared in British and in foreign law journals. The publisher, Sweet & Maxwell Ltd, issues a yearly cumulation titled *Current Law Yearbook*.

Index to Legal Periodicals, a monthly published in New York by the H. W. Wilson Company, covering articles in UK and Commonwealth law journals as well as American journals.

Popular Medical Index

This helps one find articles and books on health and medical subjects, in both specialized and lay sources. Subject headings are expressed largely in popular terms rather than in Latin-based medical wording. The editors list fifty periodicals as 'most frequently quoted in the index', adding that 'many others are scanned' for inclusion of relevant articles. The index also carries references to most newly published books in the field of popular medicine.

The professional journals most frequently quoted in the index include such titles as the *British Medical Journal*, the *Lancet*, the *General Practitioner* and *Nursing Times*. The index also includes significant articles from a few general-circulation magazines such as *Good Housekeeping*, *Parents* and *Woman's Own*. The *Popular Medical Index* is issued quarterly with an annual cumulation and first appeared in 1978. It is published by Mede publishing and is edited by Sally Knight, MLA. The index carries this most helpful notice about the references it lists: 'If you have any difficulty in obtaining an item please contact the editor.'

Research Index – Finance

Issued fortnightly, each edition of the *Research Index* is a comprehensive reference to articles and news items of financial interest appearing in more than a hundred periodicals and the national newspapers during the previous two weeks. Cumulations are issued quarterly. The index is divided into two sections, one being alphabetical under subject-matter headings; the other is arranged alphabetically by the name of the company mentioned. The *Research Index* is published by Business Surveys Ltd.

Répertoire International de la Littérature de l'Art
(International Repertory of the Literature of Art) (RILA)

Published semi-annually since 1975, RILA is a massive, detailed guide to worldwide literature on western art in all media from late antiquity (fourth century) to the present. It indexes all types of publications: books, periodical articles, conference proceedings, Festschriften, collected essays, exhibition catalogues, museum publications and doctoral dissertations. Most entries include an abstract that describes the item briefly.

RILA is produced by an international editorial committee that draws on specialists from the Courtauld Institute of Art in London, institutions in America and six European countries. RILA is a bibliographic service of the J. Paul Getty Trust.

Discussions were under way in 1986 to produce a common art database that would merge RILA with the Répertoire d'Art et d'Archéologie (RAA), which has been issued in France since 1910. It was expected that the planned new bibliography to come from the RILA–RAA merger would be quarterly and be bilingual, with abstracts appearing in either French or English, and with a full index in both languages.

It is useful to consult periodicals at both levels – the general and the specialized. In most cases the researcher should first consult the British Humanities Index to find references in general circulation periodicals. After that you should consult one or more of the specialized indexes in order to find more detailed information written for the specialized readership. General circulation periodicals frequently carry articles and illustrations of the highest quality, written by leading authorities, and benefiting from good editing. Broad conclusions and summaries which are clear to lay readers are usually plainly stated. On the other hand, articles in some specialized journals are often strong on detail and documentation, but may be obscurely written, poorly edited and not illustrated.

One should remember that the dividing line between these specialized indexes follows the subject matter of the periodical – not the subject matter of the particular article. Thus, an article on the education of engineers appearing in an engineering magazine would be listed in *Current Technology Today* and in the *Research Index* (both of which index engineering magazines) – but may not appear in the *British Education Index*.

Outside London you may have to search a bit among the city, university and specialized libraries to find those that carry the indexes you need. And you may have to search even further for libraries that carry some of the specialized periodicals to which the index entries refer you. Be certain, therefore, to consult the introduction of each index to see whether the publisher offers to supply copies of the listed periodicals for a reasonable fee. (See also Interlibrary Loan.)

Help at the Bookshop

A good nearby bookshop can be a help in research, especially when it is closer than the library, or if it is open when the library is closed. Aside from the fact that experienced booksellers know their merchandise and can put their hands on a given title fast, they always keep certain reference books to help them order and sell books – and the researcher can use these to advantage. On request a bookshop assistant will usually produce them for your inspection.

Perhaps the most useful of these is **British Books in Print** (*BBIP*), a listing issued in two volumes. Booksellers are most likely to keep the printed volumes where they are available for use by customers. In *BBIP* researchers can find in one place a list of all books now on sale (the publishing industry uses the term 'in print') under a particular subject, as well as the full name of the author, exact title, and other information that they may lack. By cross-checking the list of books in *BBIP* against the bibliography already compiled you can determine what other books are on sale that you had not known about.

BBIP combines author, title and subject entries in one alphabetical listing, which can be confusing at first until one is used to the system. Listings under an author's name can be found readily. But title entries and subject entries can be mixed, depending on their precise wording. For example, books by a writer named 'Blood' are found together. But books about blood disease and those with 'blood' as the first word of the title can be intertwined, and one needs patience to sort them out.

Reference libraries usually have *British Books in Print*, but it is often kept in a place convenient to the staff, rather than where readers can readily find and use it. In addition to *BBIP* your local bookseller should be able to refer to the *Bookseller* and other trade papers, *Paperbacks in Print* or *International Books in Print*, as well as publishers' catalogues.

A Low-Cost Home Reference Collection

In steering a course between wasting time and wasting money, we have found that it pays to buy a certain number of inexpensive reference books so that we can have them on the desk, and to consult others in the library. Of course, each researcher discovers his or her own needs and use-patterns, and each buys reference materials of particular value to them. But for general use we suggest the following reference books:

Whitaker's Almanack

This is the standard British 'book of facts', published annually since 1869, and sold widely in both a soft cover shorter edition and a full-length edition. *Whitaker's Almanack* is the best available compilation of specific information in many fields, and has been at the right hand of thousands of journalists and editors for decades. In it one can find answers to who/what/when/where questions of all sorts on government, history, geography, science, the arts, agriculture, and more categories than one can imagine. As a source of hard facts in hundreds of fields, a *Whitaker's Almanack* at hand can save the researcher many a trip to the library or search in other books.

The strength of *Whitaker's Almanack* lies in its detailed index, which contains nearly 20,000 references to general subject headings and to specific names. The shorter edition (about 700 pages) is roughly half the length of the complete edition, and costs about half as much. The index, however, is the same in both editions, which can frustrate the buyer of the shorter version who discovers that the needed information is in the complete edition, just out of reach at the moment.

Pears Cyclopaedia

Shorter than *Whitaker's Almanack* and somewhat cheaper, *Pears Cyclopaedia* is a reference annual that emphasizes summaries of recent events on a worldwide scale. Thus, it can help researchers quickly pinpoint the date of an event, from which they can then proceed to detailed accounts elsewhere. The historical section outlines important events by date throughout human history. *Pears Cyclopaedia* is divided into major sections by subject, each of which has its own table of contents. It is published by Pelham Books Ltd and was first issued in 1897.

Vacher's Parliamentary Companion

Despite its title, *Vacher's Parliamentary Companion* is a handy guide to all ministries of government as well as to Parliament and its members. Because it is revised quarterly and issued in soft cover, Vacher's is more likely to be up to date than other printed guides to Parliament and government, although in some sections it is less detailed. An annual subscription for four issues costs considerably less than the four quarterly books bought separately. (See also *International Yearbook and Statesman's Who's Who*.)

Getting Library Discards for Yourself

Many libraries, especially well-financed company libraries, make it a practice to discard superseded reference books when a new edition reaches them. They may do so both because of lack of shelf space and because they are interested in current information only. However, the next-to-last edition of most serial reference books, particularly annuals, can be highly useful to the individual researcher, because most of the information in them is sufficiently up to date for the purposes of research.

It is therefore well worth the time and trouble to make contact with a co-operative librarian in charge of a special library with a policy of discarding superseded editions, and arrange that the books be given to you instead of being thrown out. When one considers the price of reference books such as *Who's Who*, cementing a friendly relationship with a librarian to whom you offer a disposal service is most advantageous.

Biographical Research: Basic Steps

Tracking down information about people, living or dead, is

a fascinating branch of research, but you can waste a great deal of time if you do not go about it the right way. It is usually most productive to go first to the most general sources of information, and later to the more specific sources. It is best to follow this order, lest in your desire to get down to particulars, you miss something important about the subject. Among the first sources to consult are these:

Who's Who
This has been published annually since 1849. It is the best single guide to living notable individuals in the UK. However, the user should remember both that entries are based on questionnaires filled out by the subjects, so no information that the subject considers uncomplimentary is likely to be included; and that some notables do not fill out questionnaires. In some of these cases the editors may research and write an original biographical sketch if they believe that an omission would impair the usefulness of the book for reference purposes. There are also volumes called *Who Was Who*, which contain details for individuals who died between 1897 and 1980.

Other volumes in the *Who's Who* series include: *Who's Who in the World*, the *International Who's Who*, *Who's Who in America* (many other countries have their own *Who's Who* as well), the *International Yearbook and Statesman's Who's Who*, and *Who's Who in International Organizations*.

Dictionary of National Biography (DNB)
DNB is probably the most complete source of biographical information specific to Britain. (See p. 50 for more information.)

Current Biography

Published by H. W. Wilson Company since 1940, this is the next best general source of information on important personalities, and on those now dead who were written about when still living. The index in each volume extends back to the start of the decade only. (For instance, the 1966 volume index covers 1961–6). However, a *Current Biography Cumulated Index* covers the years 1940–70, and your library may have acquired a copy of the separate index. Some individuals whose careers spanned more than one decade have been written about more than once (for example, Dwight D. Eisenhower), so for information on such people you must check the indexes with care. The great value of *Current Biography* lies in its editorial independence of its subjects. Each biographical article, averaging 2,000 words, is written by the Wilson staff from information gathered from a variety of sources, both critical and favourable, rather than from the biographee alone. A short bibliography is supplied, enabling the researcher to locate further material on the subject. *Current Biography* claims to be international in its coverage but in practice it tends to be strongly biased towards American subjects.

Encyclopaedia Britannica

Along with other encyclopaedias this can also provide useful information. It hardly needs stating that encyclopaedias such as *Britannica* (as well as *Americana*, *Chambers's*, *Collier's* and *Compton's*, etc.) contain many biographical articles. What researchers frequently overlook is that *Britannica* ends each biographical article with a bibliography, from which you can quickly obtain references to the best books on the subject. For brief identification of names and people, and for condensed biographical information, the one-volume *Columbia Encyclopaedia* is a great time-saver.

Card Catalogue in a Reference Library

A standard step early on in biographical research is to check the card catalogue of a reference library under the subject's name, to find whatever books about that person, written by them or about them, are available. To find additional current books by or about the subject that are not held in your library, consult *British Books in Print* (see p. 31), considering the person as a subject indexed by last name. Books by or about living people, especially those in politics, sports and entertainment, are pouring from the presses today. It therefore pays to look to see if one has been published on a young, newly prominent person.

Obituaries

Newspapers and magazine obituaries are good sources of biographical material about people who were not national notables. The key to all obituaries is finding the date of death, then going to the files of local newspapers in the library, as well as to publications of organizations with which the subject was connected (clubs, unions, professional societies, etc.).

The *Times Index* and *The New York Times Index* (see p. 23) are both valuable in determining the death date of people of stature in the UK and USA. In 1970 *The New York Times Index* published *The New York Times Obituaries Index* as a key to finding the right obituary among more than 350,000 published in the newspaper since 1858.

Researchers should not automatically accept obituaries as gospel truth. They are just useful guides to the facts, which the reader must follow-up and check. Newspaper obituaries may be written against a demanding daily dead-line, and the writers may have to rely on distraught family members for much of their information on the recently deceased. The general outline is usually correct, but the specifics are invariably prone to error. Magazine obituaries, which are written more slowly, are usually more reliable than those in daily newspapers.

Periodical Indexes
Biographical material ranging from the most general kind of magazine article to the most specific and parochial can be found in the *British Humanities Index* (see p. 24) or its American counterpart, the *Readers' Guide to Periodical Literature* (see p. 25), and in other more specialized indexes to magazines. The same is true of *The Times Index* and *The New York Times Index* (see p. 23). For a general framework you can profitably look first under the subject's name in the *British Humanities Index* or *The Times Index*; but much more biographical detail can be extracted from the specialized journals and magazines in the fields of the subject's life and work. This is particularly the case with obituary articles in learned-society journals. These are often written by a close colleague who knew the subject more intimately than any journalist, and may often write things in the obituary that had not been published before.

No Reference Source is Complete – or Perfect

The researcher should not have blind faith that a reference book, directory, list or any other printed source of information is complete or free from errors. This is particularly true of biographical directories and lists of organizations. With but few exceptions, such printed sources depend on co-operation between the editors preparing them and those being listed. Directories are usually compiled by a solicitation system, under which editors mail out forms to those they believe should be listed in a directory, asking the latter to fill out the forms and return them.

For various reasons – such as negligence, or absence from their previous address, or reluctance to be listed in print – some who are solicited do not reply, with the result that they may not appear in the next issue of the directory. The efficiency of the editors in following up those who do not respond to the first solicitation varies. But none can be 100 per cent efficient in extracting information from all, and the editors may have failed to send forms to some who should be listed. Therefore, it is a mistake to draw any conclusions from the fact that a person or organization does not appear in a given directory.

As for accuracy of entries in a directory, the researcher should remember that the content of each entry is controlled by the one who sends in the reply to the editors' inquiry. Directory editors do very little editing of the responses they receive. Honours and degrees can be claimed that embellish the truth. Facts that might tarnish the image of the one listed can be discreetly omitted – such as a criminal record or a resignation in disgrace – or the person responding for an organization may make mistakes based on ignorance. Printed reference sources such as directories have their limitations, therefore, which the researcher should bear in mind.

Professional Tips on Note-Taking

Everyone has, at some point, taken notes on what they have read, seen or heard, but there are both good and bad ways to take notes. Here are a number of tips that can help you avoid errors and loss of time.

Thoroughness
Don't make your notes so cryptic that some time later you

will be in doubt as to exactly what the notes mean. Avoid writing notes that you alone can understand. If you use symbols or abbreviations, write down a key to their meanings for later reference. Do not rely too much on memory because it has a nasty habit of failing us at times!

System

Organize your notes into a system according to your intended use of the material – not just according to its source. Make sure you record the source of every note, because you may want to return to it later to check for accuracy or to pick up more material. It is often best to put notes on only one subject on a sheet of paper. You are then free to shuffle the sheets around in order to get them in the order you want them for use. However, in some circumstances it may be better to write your notes all on the same sheet of paper in order to maintain fluency – you can always reorganize them at a later date.

It is sometimes more convenient to use index cards rather than individual sheets or scraps of paper, which run the risk of being overlooked or lost. (The extra cost of buying record cards is minor, and well worth the expenditure.) Another advantage is that additional material on the same subject can be added later on separate record cards which can then be clipped together and kept in a card index box. If a given note can be used under more than one heading, place a cross-file note (See Also) under the second heading, and mark it with a reminder that you have placed the first copy elsewhere. In this way you will be reminded that the note is in two places, and you can avoid repeating yourself when you finally decide where to use the material. However, this system is not really appropriate for extensive note-taking.

Bibliographical notes

Note down the full data on books consulted or sought in

research to avoid confusion with other books having similar titles, or different editions, or authors with the same or similar names. A bibliographical note such as, *History of Europe*, by Smith is worthless. There are too many library catalogue cards starting with the words *History of Europe* and countless authors with the last name Smith. However, after you have identified a book with precision in your notes you can best save time by referring to it by the surname of the author, because book titles are longer than surnames and there are more similarities among titles.

When first consulting a book, note down the author, title, city of publication, publisher and year of publication. These are the required items in a formal bibliography. If you write them down when the book is in your hands you will not waste time later chasing these details. It is also worth while noting which library you found the book in.

Negative results
You should note down negative results – failure to find anything worth noting – from a source, as an *aide mémoire* for later use. Otherwise, the absence of any notes from a potential research source may lead you to investigate it a second time.

Mechanics of note-taking
Notes can be taken most easily by hand. It is well worth developing the skill of being able to print neatly and quickly so that your notes are always clear. If you are a fast typist you may find it less arduous to take notes on a typewriter rather than by hand. Typing can be faster, and there is no difficulty reading your notes later. If your library permits the use of a silent portable typewriter or wordprocessor, the investment is well worth it.

N.B. It is a good idea to get into the habit of taking notes only on one side of a sheet of paper. It is all too easy to forget to look at the reverse side of a sheet. Clean out your notes regularly; remove outdated items and those found to be incorrect. It is better to have a compact set of useful notes than to lose your useful pages among a mass of notes that you will never use again.

Public Relations Sources

Public relations people and offices can be of great help to the researcher. They go under various names – public relations (often PR for short), publicity, public information (the term used in government), press relations officers and, in embassies, press attaché. Whatever the name, these are the people and offices whose job it is to supply information to the press and the public on behalf of an organization, institution or individual.

In recent years the PR function has become so important that in many cases the person best equipped to supply information about an institution is the PR director – not the chairman or chief executive. Most academics have not accepted this fact, so very few lecturers tell students how to use the PR network. One reason is that there is an academic prejudice against PR sources as unscholarly. This prejudice is beside the point, because no one seeking information from a PR source should leave his or her critical faculties behind. Researchers should be at least as careful in accepting what they are told as they would be about statements read in a journal article or a book.

This caution is relevant when dealing with the public information officer of a university or a government department, just as it is with the PR person of a manufacturing company or an airline. It is the researcher's job to screen out what is valid and factual from that which is distorted, inflated or untrue. If you recognize that you should count on the PR sources for only certain parts of the story, and if you can discount the rest, then the PR source can save you a great deal of time in assembling those valid parts. In summary, do not overlook the service that PR sources can give, but always remember that they have a vested interest in the information they are providing.

When making the first contact with an organization avoid terminology differences by asking for 'the public relations officer, or whoever acts in that capacity'. This approach usually gets results. A second step, particularly with large companies, is to find out whether it does its own PR work or employs an outside PR agency. If the latter, you should find out which public relations agency represents the company, and then find the account executive at the agency who is responsible for that client.

The PR agency will usually supply the inquiring student, writer or anyone else with information because doing so is evidence of work performed on the client's behalf. If, in approaching an agency, you indicate how you intend to use the client's name in a favourable way, so much the better. Agency people willingly give their time to answer questions because that is what they are paid to do. A PR person can save you much effort by supplying reports, texts, statistics, pictures and bibliographies.

Frequently in the case of a big company or institution no one outside its national headquarters can tell you whether a PR agency represents it, and if so, which one. If you cannot find out easily through local company sources, consult *Hollis Press and Public Relations Annual*, which lists press contacts, official and public sources of information and PR consultancies as well as a wealth of other valuable information. For information about American companies or organizations you should consult *O'Dwyer's Directory of Public Relations Firms*. Listings in this annual directory are broken down by client name, by type of PR firm and by city. A companion annual, *O'Dwyer's Directory of Corporate Communications*, is organized by companies and gives details of their internal PR staff. Because PR is a fast-changing business, it is always wise to double-check discreetly to make certain that a given company is still a client of an agency or that a person named as the public relations director is still in the same position.

The 'At-the-Binders' Gap

Libraries frequently remove from the shelves the issues of magazines and journals that are one to two years old and send them out for binding in hardcover volumes. Unless the library keeps a second set of unbound issues for use during that 'at-the-binders' gap, there may be several weeks during which you would not have access to the issues. The most common practice is for magazines to be sent to the binders when they are no longer current, and when copies covering the last full year can be left on the shelves.

To avoid fruitless trips to the library to consult magazines and journals that are from one to three years old, you can ask the reference librarian to tell you whether the issues you need are on the shelves or at the bindery. Most librarians keep an accurate 'at-the-binders' list at the service desk, and can answer this query at once. But they rarely volunteer the information before you have spent your time looking for missing issues.

INTERMEDIATE TECHNIQUES

The research methods and sources of information presented in this chapter are those that most researchers will need as they progress further in their research and become more accomplished at accessing information. Again, readers would do well to bear in mind that the frequency with which they will need to use these techniques will depend on the type of research they are doing.

Access to Library Stacks

Reference libraries can be invaluable to the researcher as certain reference libraries receive a copy of every book published in the United Kingdom. There are six such libraries, known as copyright libraries, which have received one free copy of every book that has been published in the United Kingdom since the eighteenth century. The copyright libraries are: the British Library in London, the Bodleian Library in Oxford, the Cambridge University Library, the National Library of Wales in Aberystwyth, the National Library of Scotland in Edinburgh and Trinity College Library in Dublin.

Although admission to the British Library and other major reference libraries is free, readers' tickets are only issued to researchers who cannot conduct their research elsewhere. In the case of a student the application for a reader's ticket must be endorsed by a college tutor. However, researchers who need access to the library for only one or two days can obtain a pass with little or no difficulty.

Most reference libraries require you to fill in a request slip for the books you wish to use and an attendant then retrieves them from the shelves. However, in some reference libraries and in almost all references sections of ordinary libraries the readers are free to search among the stacks themselves. Gaining access to the stacks is of great value to the researcher in a library where books are catalogued and arranged by subject because:

· You can often find books you need more quickly by going to the shelves than by filing request slips at the service desk and waiting for books to be delivered

- You can find additional useful books that you would not find from the card catalogue

- You will sometimes find books you have ordered, but which stack attendants overlook because they are misplaced on the shelves.

By consulting the subject heading in the library card catalogue, you can find the reference number under which books on that subject are listed and arranged on the shelves. You can fill out request slips for every book under that heading, send for them, examine them, and retain the most useful ones for study. But it is much more efficient to find the call number, then go to the place in the stacks where the books under that number are shelved, and examine them in place. It may be a dusty business, carried out under poor lighting. But it pays, because you can examine and reject a dozen books quickly and walk out to the reading room with two or three that you consider the best – in terms of recent publication date, quality of the index, illustrations, readable type, clarity of style and coverage of the subject.

A second advantage of stack-searching is that it permits you to search the adjoining shelves, where books on closely allied subjects (with slightly different reference numbers) can be found. For instance, biographies of astronomers may adjoin histories of astronomy, technical books on astronomical instruments, and bound volumes of astronomy journals. Because these various classifications of book are close at hand, you may come upon useful material that you would not have found so readily by using the card catalogue.

In a big reference library a book may be misshelved just a few places away from its correct numerical position, with the result that the stack attendant may not find it. It is then reported 'not on shelf' to the reader who ordered it. If the book is reported 'not on shelf' on a second attempt another day, you can profitably take time to look for yourself in the stacks, close to where the book should be shelved. For one thing, your motivation is greater than the stack attendant's; and you may know something about the appearance of the book, and so recognize it more easily. However, do not be surprised if you are denied access to the shelves in large libraries. In these you have no choice but to be patient and persevere.

For researchers who feel it is essential that they have free access to the stacks it is worth while taking out a subscription to the London Library. The library holds books on the humanities, literature and the arts, and on science publications where they are of historical interest. Various types of subscription are available. The annual subscription (in 1990 it is £80) entitles you to take out ten books at any one time, or fifteen books if you live more than twenty miles away. For overseas visitors who are in the country for up to four months a full borrowing rights subscription costing £37.50 is available. For those researchers who do not require borrowing rights a reading room subscription costing £10 per month is available.

Know the Reference Book Catalogues

The best way to keep up with most useful general reference books and services, many of which are updated annually, is to read the latest reference catalogue. The two most important of these are *Walford's Guide to Reference Materials* (see p. 77) and Gavin L. Higgens's *Printed Reference Materials* (see below), both published by the Library Association. Both of these publications are invaluable for enabling the researcher to identify sources of information and to gain some indication of how potentially useful the sources are.

Printed Reference Materials is published specifically for libraries and therefore should be available at most good libraries, although you may have to ask the librarian if you can see a copy. The other major publisher of reference materials worth checking is A. and C. Black, London, who produce the *Who's Who* series.

Indexes to Newspapers Other Than The Times

Beyond the index to *The Times*, there are several other published indexes to daily newspapers in English that have been available in reference libraries for several years. The British Library Colindale Library, Colindale Avenue, London NW9 5HE has a large collection of these indexes. Other major collections are in the national or university libraries in Edinburgh, Birmingham, Manchester, Oxford, Cambridge, Dublin and Aberystwyth. A reference librarian can help you locate the nearest library where you can consult the newspaper indexes you require. In any library it is always worth while to inquire into the complete list of newspaper indexes available there, because from time to time local newspapers have produced their own indexes for a few years, then abandoned the effort, and only a few copies are to be found today. The library may have gaps in its collection of a particular index because the subscription was dropped, and then resumed, or because the newspaper stopped producing it for a period.

These indexes frequently lead one to information not carried in *The Times*, largely because of their local viewpoint and emphasis. Logically, Canadian newspapers would carry more news on the political career of Prime Minister Pierre Trudeau than *The Times* would offer, and *The New York Times* or the *Wall Street Journal* would have more news of New York financial affairs. Among the newspaper indexes carried in British libraries are:

Newcastle Morning Herald, since 1861

Financial Times, 1913–20; and since 1981

Glasgow Herald, 1907–20; and since 1981

Argus, Melbourne, 1846–54; 1910–48

Sydney Morning Herald and *Sydney Mail*, 1927–48; *Sydney Morning Herald* and *Sunday Herald* 1949–57

Canadian News Index, since 1977. An integrated index of articles in seven newspapers published in Calgary, Toronto, Halifax, Montreal, Vancouver and Winnipeg

The New York Times, since 1851. This is the oldest American newspaper index and is the one most widely available in Britain. It has a number of useful offshoots, such as sub-indexes to obituaries, proper names and theatrical reviews, each covering many years and saving the researcher a great deal of time

Wall Street Journal, since 1955. Concentrates on business and economic news, and carries a separate corporate-name index

Washington Post, since 1971

Los Angeles Times, Chicago Tribune, since 1972.

With each passing year it is likely that more newspaper indexes will be published in print or on microfilm, because the technique of compiling and reproducing them is steadily being refined. So do not hesitate to ask whether a new newspaper index has appeared since you last inquired.

Biographical Reference: A Few Useful Books

There are so many published biographical reference

materials that it would be futile to try to list one tenth of them in this book. The few described below are selected because they are among the most widely distributed in libraries, and therefore the easiest to find, and because they are among the biographical source books of most general use. Researchers looking for limited biographical material will find them the most convenient source of information, but those digging beneath the surface of things should consider these books only as useful aids at the start.

Biography Index

Published by H. W. Wilson Co. since 1946, this is a highly useful index that brings together, under the subject's name, references to biographical material appearing in about 2,400 periodicals indexed in other Wilson indexes; in current books of biography in English; in obituaries; and in incidental biographical material from otherwise non-biographical books. In brief, the editors of the *Biography Index* have assembled many references, saving the researcher who uses the index a great deal of time. It is published quarterly, and bound in annual and three-yearly cumulations. The *Biography Index* claims to be international in its coverage, but in practice it tends to be heavily biased towards American material.

Dictionary of National Biography

Called the DNB by librarians, this first appeared between 1885 and 1901 in sixty-three volumes (currently in twenty-two volumes), and has since been augmented by supplements every decade. It is published by the Oxford University Press. Like the *Dictionary of American Biography*, this massive work does not include biographies of living persons. It contains more than 32,000 biographies of people who lived in Britain and the British Commonwealth. There is also a *Concise Dictionary of National Biography*, in two volumes, published in 1952 (to 1900) and in 1961 (to 1950). There is also a *Chronological and Occupational Index to the DNB*.

Dictionary of American Biography (DAB)

This American counterpart of the DNB is edited under the auspices of the American Council of Learned Societies and published in twenty volumes between 1928 and 1936 with an index volume and five supplements, published up to 1977. A newer reprint edition contains the original twenty volumes plus the supplements. The DAB contains no living subjects among its 16,000 biographees, all of whom were Americans.

Finding Periodicals on Particular Subjects

There are times in research when one wants to find out whether there are any periodicals devoted to a particular subject or interest, and if so, which are the most significant ones. Two directories can provide the answers: *Willing's Press Guide*, published by Thomas Skinner Directories, and *Benn's Media Directory*, UK volume, published by Benn's Business Information Services Ltd. (Benn's also publish an international volume, covering the press worldwide in 195 countries.) Both are annuals that have been published for more than a century. They define periodicals broadly, and so list small and large circulation periodicals, specialized and general interest, weeklies, annuals and frequencies in between. *Willing's* lists more than 7,500 periodicals of less than annual frequency, and nearly 2,100 annuals. *Benn's* list is comparable, and includes up to thirty words of description and readership details for each title. Because errors are bound to creep into the production of such massive reference books, the researcher would do well to consult both directories to discover any omissions or recent changes. Both offer such essential information as the field of concentration of the listed periodical, year of foundation, address, editor's name and circulation figures.

Both directories include a detailed classified index enabling the user to find all listed periodicals devoted to a specific field of interest. However, one should be careful in using these classified indexes and not jump to conclusions about the extent of any one subject heading. For instance, *Willing's* has a fairly short list of periodicals under the heading of 'Sports', but it has separate lists of periodicals under 'Football', 'Golf', 'Tennis' and 'Yachting'.

These two directories help you find periodicals you have never seen, and learn a good deal about them, in subject-fields in which you know little or nothing. You can then hunt them down in a special library or try to obtain sample copies from the publisher.

Anbar Abstracting Services – Business Management

Anbar Management Publications covers a journal base of more than 250 periodicals carrying articles of interest to business managers, and issues five services indexed and organized by subject. Each entry includes an abstract of forty to a hundred words in length. Journals covered, in addition to the British, include significant ones from the USA, the Commonwealth countries and Western Europe. Each of the five Anbar abstracting services is prepared in association with an authoritative British Institute in the relevant field. The services are:

* *Accounting and Data Processing Abstracts* – published in association with the Institute of Chartered Accountants in England and Wales

* *Marketing and Distribution Abstracts* – in association with the Institute of Marketing

- *Personnel and Training Abstracts* – in association with the Institute of Personnel Management

- *Top Management Abstracts* – in association with the British Institute of Management (BIM).

- *Work Study & O & M Abstracts* – in association with the Institute of Management Services.

A notable feature of the Anbar service is that it helps people to obtain a copy of the article(s) they need, if they cannot find it elsewhere. Each issue of the Anbar abstracting journals gives the names and addresses of the co-operating institute libraries through which copies of articles are supplied for a modest fee, and subscribers to Anbar's comprehensive service may borrow articles from the library.

Is There a Directory That Can Help?

In locating organizations or individuals who can supply information in a research project, it can be most helpful to consult a directory of the right sort that lists such groups or people. If it is not known whether there is a directory of potential sources, especially in a field that is new, a good directory to turn to is *Current British Directories*, a reference book that has been issued every three years since 1953 by CBD Research Ltd and is found in many reference libraries. Running to nearly 600 pages, this directory of British directories describes some 2,500 specialized directories of all sorts covering industries, trades, professions, hobbies, sport and other categories. A detailed subject index helps one find the listing of one or more directories in a given field. It also lists 250 local directories of places in the UK, and has a special fifty-page section listing British publishers and the directories they issue.

A useful note in the introduction headed 'Where to consult directories' lists seven libraries in London that have substantial collections of directories to which the reader may be referred. It also offers practical advice on locating the needed directories outside London. A companion volume, *Current European Directories*, describes directories published on the continent of Europe.

Associations – Key to Finding Specialists

The British are a nation of specialists, with many diverse interests. People with particular interests in common, whether they are hobbyists, professionals or in business, group together. They form clubs, professional societies, business organizations and trade associations through which they can pursue their common interests in an organized way. They become acquainted with one another. and learn what their fellow members are doing. If a researcher wants to investigate a subject in which there are hundreds, even thousands, of specialists, it is highly useful to get in touch with the association of which they are likely to be members. (See also Information Networks at your Service, p. 61). This is made easy by consulting the *Directory of British Associations and Associations in Ireland*, which is available in most reference libraries. First issued in 1965, this directory is issued every two or three years. The eighth edition appearing in early 1986. It includes a subject index that enables the researcher to find associations concerned with a particular subject, even if the exact name of the association is not known. For instance, a researcher looking under 'Clocks' is referred to 'Horology', where eight associations concerned with timepieces will be found. Similar cross-references connect 'Apiculture' with 'Bees' and 'Beekeeping', and 'Arachnology' with 'Spiders'.

The main part of the directory lists more than 6,000 associations. Each entry includes all or most of the following: date of establishment; address, telephone and telex number; name of secretary or chief executive with designation of office held; branches and groups; type of association and purpose; membership data including number of individuals, firms and organizations; activities; affiliations and publications, with frequency and price. The publisher of the directory is CBD Research Ltd.

The amount of detail in these entries makes it possible for the researcher not only to locate associations but also to distinguish the dominant and significant ones from the minor ones. Among the possible benefits from making contact with an association are: finding authorities to interview (such as the association executive, secretary or other officers); reaching the association library and possibly the librarian; finding the back files of the association records; obtaining the association's publications, which may be virtually unknown to non-members; locating veteran members with long memories of past events; and finding members in your part of the country who can serve as sources of information if the association headquarters are at an inconvenient distance. You probably could not find them so easily in any other way.

CBD Research Ltd also publishes the *Directory of European Associations* in two volumes giving details of industrial, trade and professional associations, and scientific and learned societies in all countries of Europe, excluding Great Britain and Ireland.

Government As an Information Source

Because Parliament and the various ministries of the national government are concerned in some way with many of our activities and interests, they are a source of detailed information on a far greater scale than many laypersons realize. The trick for the researcher in tapping these sources is to find out which individuals, which agencies and which government publications would be most useful. In order to do this you need to find out first which members of Parliament and which Parliamentary committees take a particular interest in a given subject, and will therefore be able to guide the reseacher in the right direction; and second, which government officers and ministries are responsible for administration in a given field. In some cases the path to the right committees and agencies is quite clear from their name. But in other cases there is no simple route, and the search for government sources may lead to several individuals and organizations, each having a bearing on part of the subject.

A useful book to assist the researcher in reaching Parliamentary and Government sources is *Dod's Parliamentary Companion*, an annual published since 1832, and widely distributed in libraries and among people working actively in politics. It contains biographical data on members of both Houses of Parliament, and photographs of many members, as well as membership of select committees of both houses. An especially useful recent addition to *Dod's* is a section titled 'MPs' Political & Social Interests', organized by subject. Here one can find the names of those MPs most likely to take an interest in an inquiry on a subject that is close to their own hearts.

Although most of *Dod's* is concerned with Parliament, it also carries lists of government and public offices of the UK, the judiciary and many other organizations and office-holders whom the researcher may wish to reach with inquiries.

Looking in on Parliament with Hansard

Hansard, which is the official report of the House of Commons and the House of Lords and is printed daily when Parliament is sitting, is a highly useful source of information on matters of current interest as well as a goldmine for historians and biographers. Named after an early editor of the proceedings of Parliament in the nineteenth century, *Hansard* is now produced under the authority of Parliament and is distributed through Her Majesty's Stationery Office. It is available to researchers in reference libraries and in private libraries of associations, companies and others who subscribe to it.

The main body of *Hansard*, both *Hansard–Lords* and *Hansard–Commons*, is a verbatim transcript of speeches given in both Houses of Parliament. Proceedings are taken down in shorthand by reporters working in relays, then are transcribed, set in type, printed and distributed within a few hours. There is a separate book for each House each day. The events reported in a given day's issue of *Hansard* end at 10.30 p.m. Debate after that hour is continued in the *Hansard* of the following day.

What makes Hansard so valuable in research is its index, which is compiled fortnightly during a session of Parliament, and is cumulated after the session adjourns into one alphabetical index for the entire session (usually November to June). The index covers both the debates and the answers given by ministers to written questions submitted by Members of Parliament. It is itemized both by Members' names and by subject. One can therefore find in the index under the name of a Member all speeches by that Member, questions asked by the Member and even references by others to that Member. Likewise, under a given subject in the index it is easy to find the debates on that subject and action taken in reference to it. And it is sometimes especially interesting to find from the *Hansard* index that nothing at all was said or done on a given subject that became of major importance just a short while later.

Unlike most printed reference sources, *Hansard* is numbered by columns rather than by pages – which can be confusing until a reader discovers this arrangement. The numbering system is dual, there being one series of numbers for the columns of Parliamentary debates and ministers' oral answers to questions, and a separate series of numbers for the columns titled 'Written Answers to Questions'. In the index to *Hansard*, references to written answers are marked **W** after the column number. Finding the debate on a given subject quickly is aided by short running heads carried at the top of each page.

The index to *Hansard* is limited to a cumulation of only one session of Parliament. However, the rapid development of computerization may soon make it both technically and economically feasible to combine the *Hansard* index into longer periods of more than one year.

Her Majesty's Stationery Office

As the publishing house for the national government, the Publications Division of Her Majesty's Stationery Office (HMSO) produces a great variety of printed matter valuable to the serious researcher. HMSO began in 1786 as supplier of such office requisites as sand, sealing wax, quills and red tape to Parliament and government departments, adding the publication function along the way. It now produces some 8,000 new titles a year and has about 40,000 in print, covering a range of subjects as broad as the interests of Parliament and those of the government departments, which in effect means the interests of the British people. Topics vary from Acts, Bills, White Papers and *Hansard* to popular guides on long-distance footpaths and historic monuments, and to books and pamphlets for the pharmacist, archaeology, gardening or photography. When carrying out research in any subject in which it is conceivable that a government department might take an interest, it is worthwhile to see whether HMSO has published material that would be helpful.

HMSO maintains its own bookshops in six cities: London, Birmingham, Bristol, Manchester, Belfast and Edinburgh, where one can consult HMSO catalogues, examine many of the publications, and buy those that are in stock. Items not in stock can be ordered for delivery by post. In addition, there are bookshops in forty cities in the UK that serve as HMSO agents by carrying the catalogues and a number of the most popular HMSO titles for sale, and deal with customers' queries. HMSO also has more than fifty overseas agents around the world that offer a similar service. Lists of all these bookshops, with addresses, are carried in many HMSO catalogues.

A logical first step in making use of government publications is to examine the list of twenty-seven catalogues (called *Sectional Lists of Government Publications*) to find those most likely to be useful. The catalogues are divided generally, though not precisely, into the fields of interest of the national government departments (such as Agriculture, Fisheries and Food; Department of the Environment; Royal Commission on Historical Manuscripts; British Geological Survey; and Overseas Affairs, etc). The second step is to select from the *Sectional Lists* the items one judges most likely to be of interest, then try to get a copy of each for examination to see if they are worth buying. None of the HMSO shops or agents could possibly stock all HMSO titles in print, but all can be ordered. Sometimes one can find the desired items in an HMSO shop or at a bookseller, or even at a public library, especially if it is a popular title much in demand. But if the item cannot be found conveniently, the researcher may be forced to decide whether to buy the item blind, without seeing it.

In addition to the *Sectional Lists*, HMSO issues a

number of promotional pamphlets to publicize publications that fall into a particular field of interest, such as: 'Art Books from HMSO'; 'Books for the Veterinary Profession'; 'Mother and Child Care'; and 'Britain's Architectural Heritage'. HMSO also acts as the UK sales agent for a number of important national and international bodies, including the United Nations, the European Communities and the World Health Organization, and publicizes their titles in the subject catalogues. It also places advertisements in the trade press and specialist journals. No other publisher in Great Britain makes so great an effort to acquaint the public with the wealth of material it issues in their interest.

Citizens Advice Bureaux Are Ready to Help

Anyone seeking information that is needed to solve a wide variety of problems can turn to the nearest Citizens Advice Bureau (CAB) and obtain help confidentially and free of charge. There are more than 900 CABs in Britain, staffed by well-trained men and women whose mission is to assist anyone who comes to them for help. First organized locally in 1939 to give an emergency service in time of war, the bureaux are now organized under the National Association of Citizens Advice Bureaux (NACAB), to offer information and advice on almost any subject, and to follow it up with action, to meet human needs in an increasingly complex society. CABs affiliated with NACAB handled 5,815,000 inquiries during the 1984–5 fiscal year.

The largest number of recent inquiries have concerned social security, particularly the rights of individuals under the social security regulations. Other categories of inquiry frequently brought to CABs have included: consumer, trade and business; housing, property and land; family and personal questions; employment; and administration of justice. In addition, CABs give information and advice on health, taxation, education, immigration and other matters.

To ensure that local CABs are kept up to date on the latest information, such as changes in social security legislation, or court rulings, or housing regulations, NACAB sends regularly to each bureau packets of new material updating the older printed matter. Thanks to this system, CAB workers are likely to be among the best-informed people in the community on the many rules and regulations that affect the lives of every resident of the UK.

Citizens Advice Bureaux are generally found in the business centre of the community, and are listed in telephone directories. Public libraries often have leaflets from the nearest CAB describing its services and giving its exact location. CABs affiliated with NACAB are distributed throughout England, Wales and Northern Ireland. Bureaux in Scotland are co-ordinated through the Scottish Association of Citizens Advice Bureaux (SACAB). SACAB exchanges a certain amount of printed matter with NACAB in London.

Information Networks at Your Service

In research it is often productive to pause and ask yourself: who can help me? what people, what organizations, have material that I need?

Your answer to this kind of thinking about your methods of research may lead you down highly rewarding paths to new sources of information. We call these paths 'information networks'. Here are several of them.

Newspaper Reporters and Editors
Reporters and editors of the daily and weekly newspapers throughout the UK are among the best-informed sources of information on events in their own localities. Two annual

directories are useful in finding quickly the name, address, telephone number and editor of every UK newspaper by locality: *Willing's Press Guide Directories* and *Benn's Media Directory* (UK Volume) (see p. 51). *Benn's* is the more useful to researchers in certain cases, because it gives the names and specialities of journalists on the staff of most of the national dailies and the big dailies, though not of the weeklies. Where the names are listed, it is possible for the researcher to address the reporter or editor who is responsible, for, say, drama, or business, or sport in a particular city.

Newspapers usually keep files of cuttings in their libraries, organized by subject. Frequently a newspaper will fulfill a request for background material on a specific subject – especially if it can be easily photocopied from cuttings on file. Thus, *Willing's* and *Benn's* can lead one quickly to the local newspaper specialists on many topics in all parts of the country, and to what they have written. To supplement their annual publication *Benn's* also provide a free update service for their subscribers to keep them abreast of change.

Public Relations Sources
(See p. 42.)

Trade Associations
One of the primary functions of trade associations, a loose term for groups of people and businesses engaged in the same or similar economic activity, is gathering and supplying information about the industry. Frequently trade association statistics and studies are the only definitive ones in their particular fields. Although a small amount of trade association information is confidential, for members only, most of it is open to anyone who asks.

A national trade association is best approached through

its chief executive officers, whose exact title varies widely among trade associations. Others to whom the researcher can best direct queries are the public relations director, the editor of the trade association publication, and the librarian at the association headquarters.

Sources through which to locate trade associations:

- *Directory of British Associations and Associations in Ireland* published by CBD Research Ltd, lists all existing associations by subject (see p. 54). Alternatively consult *Trade Associations and Professional Bodies in the United Kingdom* published by Gale Research International, Andover.

- *Whitaker's Almanack* is published annually by J. Whitaker, London (see p. 33). It lists various institutions and societies but does not provide the reader with very much additional information.

- *Business Pages* is compiled and published by British Telecommunications PLC, and is updated annually. The directory is published in seven regional versions and can be obtained at a cost of £7.50 each. The 'Help and Advice' section of the current edition contains all the useful addresses and telephone numbers of trade associations and federations, professional institutes, advisory bodies and Chambers of Commerce.

Local Councils and Local Councillors

Your council may have an information department which can provide you with information about local services, particularly those provided by the council itself. Your local Member of Parliament can also be of help. If you are not sure of the names of your councillor or member of Parliament, the local librarian can help.

Thompson Local Directory

This is delivered free of charge to every home within the area covered. Information presented in the directory includes:

- information about the local community; maps, lists of post-codes, details of council services, names, addresses and phone numbers of local representatives, etc.

- names, addresses and telephone numbers of all local businesses categorized by the nature of the business.

Alumni Offices

It is becoming increasingly common for universities and colleges to keep records on their alumni because alumni have become a prime source for donations. Alumni bulletins and magazines contain a wealth of biographical material unpublished elsewhere on graduates of significance, and articles by or about such people not indexed elsewhere. Therefore the alumni secretary and staff are prime sources of biographical information.

In some cases alumni secretaries protect the privacy of individuals by referring queries about a current address directly to the alumnus, to answer if he or she pleases.

Research Gold in the Filing Cabinets

A great deal of written material useful in serious research is preserved in filing cabinets in thousands of accessible places. Yet to find and use these files we must search in ways different from those used to locate material in books and periodicals. Files contain just about anything on paper. There are printed pamphlets, folders, brochures and other publications too slim to be classified as books. There are publications for limited distribution (such as the news bulletin of an organization) which do not possess copyright, are not sold through bookstores, and not listed or catalogued anywhere. Mixed in with them may be offprints of magazine articles or journal articles, pictorial material, leaflets, programmes, manuscripts that were never duplicated and scrapbooks of clippings, pictures and mementoes kept by an individual. The contents and organization of such mixed files vary from one extreme to the other.

You can waste time searching at random for files that may be highly useful to you, or you may overlook rich sources in filing cabinets that you might have found with ease. Here are several ways to locate files that seem most promising – after which you are on your own in digging into them:

Organizations

Following the rule of 'Who would care?' (see p. 8), look for organizations, associations, companies and so forth that would most likely be concerned with the subject in which you are interested. To find associations consult the *Directory of British Associations and Associations in Ireland* (see p. 54); for manufacturing companies consult *Business Pages* or *Thompson Local Directory* (p. 64). Companies generally keep their records under careful control on their own premises, but they frequently permit authorized students, biographers and historians to consult them. A company may require you to agree to a company review of what you intend to publish, as a condition for permitting you to use the files at all. In these cases you must use your diplomatic skills to make the best arrangement possible.

With associations, access to records is generally easier. A researcher should check to see if the association has kept the files of the headquarters staff, annual meetings, officers and committees dealing with the subject of the inquiry. In many cases associations are glad to open their files to a serious researcher, especially if doing so offers the promise of favourable treatment of the organization. Check also whether they have passed their back files on, perhaps for lack of storage space, to a related organization, to a parent federation, or to a library specializing in that subject. In these days of high rents in office buildings it occurs frequently that an organization cleans out its non-current files and turns them over to a nearby non-profit educational institution, such as a university library.

Special Libraries

Librarians usually refer to their file collections (other than books, periodicals and manuscripts) as 'archive material'. Occasionally when looking through the library catalogue you will come across the note 'not on shelves, ask at desk'. You will normally find that the librarian has a filing cabinet in which are kept a limited number of single-sheet documents, bibliographies prepared by the library, etc. The critical questions then are: 'how well are the files organized and indexed?' 'do they contain material specifically related to your research?' A telephone query may save you a trip; and if you have a choice, it is the better-organized collection, rather than the larger one, that is preferable for the first look. Although an alert, well-trained librarian can help you reach your research target, there is no substitute for examining the files yourself.

Public and University Libraries

Public libraries, most of which are general libraries, usually do not have large archive collections because the materials are difficult to preserve and control. One exception is material on local history, which in many cities is given to the public library, and which the library staff feels duty-bound to store, although the library is often not equipped to process it and preserve it according to professional library standards.

University libraries, like city libraries, are sometimes given files by graduates of the university and they feel it their duty to keep them, although the materials fall in a twilight zone between bound books (which are catalogued by author, title and subject) and manuscripts (which are organized by the former owner's name). The librarian will almost always be able to tell you what material is available and will usually have to retrieve it for you.

Personal Files

Whenever you find a specialist or an expert, the chances are you have found someone who keeps personal files. Individuals who have filed information diligently and well in the subject-matter field in which you are interested are worth their weight in gold — provided they are willing to share their knowledge and accumulations with you.

When you find such a person, be sure to ask whether they have kept a scrapbook of newspaper cuttings, book reviews and other excerpts from printed matter about their work. If they or a proud member of their family have collected such a scrapbook (or the equivalent in looseleaf form) and if you are given access to it, you may have hit the research jackpot, for a good scrapbook contains material that is almost impossible to duplicate by research at a later date.

Personal files are worth pursuing well after the death of the individual who kept them. Frequently surviving families do not know just what to do with the files kept by the deceased, either in the home or in the office, so they postpone a decision by simply storing them. Therefore, the attics and basements of widows and offspring are well worth the researcher's attention.

Finding the Person Who Knows

Frequently the facts we want and need to know are not in print, but we have reason to believe that someone, an expert or a specialist, has them. The research job then is to locate that person. Here are a few ways to go about locating the person or persons who can help you:

Organizations and Interest Groups

If you do not already know it, find the association to which the expert or specialist is likely to belong through the *Directory of British Associations and Associations in Ireland* (p. 54). Through the assocation, or its regional or local division in your area, or a well-informed local member, you can frequently locate someone with the special knowledge you require who is conveniently close to you.

Remember that those with particular interests or work specialities come into contact with others in their fraternity, or hear about them. So if a first referral turns out to be not what you need, one specialist can refer you to another. Doctors, for example, become members of professional associations and also join the organization (board or college) of their medical speciality. They read the medical journal articles written by their colleagues and meet them at professional meetings. Tournament-calibre tennis players meet one another on the court, and keep up with the records of competitors in their specialized journal, *World Tennis*. Serious bridge players do the same. University and school teachers know many of their colleagues in other institutions through job transfers and professional groups, and attending conferences.

Frequently an organization's membership register is in print. Searching for such printed lists, and searching the lists for the people you want, is a first step. If an organization does not have a published membership directory, the officers or staff of the group will often help locate a member from the office files if the request appears legitimate and does not violate the member's privacy.

A register of committee chairmen and committee members is highly useful in pinning down the names of those people in a national organization who have special interests and knowledge. The organization's annual report or its official publication can be a quick guide to the names of committee chairmen.

Specialized News Reporters and Editors (see p. 61)

The specialized reporter on the local newspaper, if he or she is a good one, can guide the researcher to people near at hand who are the sources for newspaper articles in business, or politics, or the courts, or medicine, or local history. The reporter or editor may therefore be a short-cut to finding the expert you need, or finding a local member of a national organization who may have its membership register, annual report, official publication and other material of help.

Business Card File

You may find that one of the most effective ways of keeping in touch with people you have met once, and who are regarded as potential sources of specialized information, is to keep a file of their business cards. Frequently after a brief or casual contact you forget the person's name but can remember that they were a certain kind of specialist, or connected with a particular organization. For this reason it is best to file the cards by subject rather than by the person's name. This enables you to call on people with a request for research help long after the initial meeting, even though you have forgotten their name in the interim. If you cannot obtain a business card write the information down on an index card and file it with the rest.

Straight from the Horse's Mouth

In research in fields where there are experts aplenty, we sometimes overlook the testimony of ordinary people – not scholars or experts in the accepted sense – who know certain limited things because they were there, personally involved, or did it themselves. The serious researcher should always seek out such witnesses because they can frequently correct a record that was distorted in the first writing, and was perpetuated by scholarly experts copying each other.

Going straight to the horse's mouth has proved especially valuable to contemporary historians and biographers, because eye-witnesses and participants have memories of things not previously in print. They have helped us get a more accurate picture, for instance, of such past events as the sinking of the *Titanic* in 1912. In addition to ordinary observers, such people as the chauffeur, the doorman, the secretary, the executive assistant and the switchboard operator observe people and events from a special viewpoint. They should therefore be considered prime sources for the researcher – as they are for the detective.

One step removed are professionals such as the doctor, lawyer, clergyman and tax accountant who have special, intimate knowledge of people of interest, and who are bound by professional ethics to keep confidences. But even with them, the passage of time permits a certain relaxation of the confidentiality rule for the sake of contributing to an accurate historical record.

Requests for Information That Get Results

When you write a letter to a potential source of research information, write in the way in which you would appreciate being written to. Especially when the recipient does not know the writer, it is unfair to put him or her to unnecessary trouble to assist you. It is also unrealistic. You are most likely to receive a satisfactory reply if you observe these rules of correspondence in research:

Be precise
Ask your sources exactly what you want from them, putting your request within the context of what you have already learned, explaining what you have already read, etc. This will help your correspondents see that all you want is a brief, precise answer, and it will avoid wasting their time supplying information you already have. For instance, do not ask an expert for a list of books to read on your subject; instead, send your bibliography and ask if there are any obvious important omissions that should be called to your attention.

Ask for printed matter
After outlining what you want to know, particularly when corresponding with public information officers and public relations people, ask if they have printed matter that would help in your research which they can send to you. If so, then you can first read what is sent and follow up later with a more precise query.

Be diplomatic
When seeking information from an expert or a Very Important Person, write a convincing explanation of why that person alone can help you. Possible ploys in correspondence might be along the lines of: 'After much study of the subject I have been unable to find any written reference to —, so I am contacting you as the only surviving person who was involved . . .', or 'I can find no reference in all your writings, the definitive ones on the subject, to —. So I would like to ask you . . .' Remember that it does no harm to flatter the expert and the VIP, if it is done discreetly and with sincerity.

Correspond with authors

Writers of books and articles frequently receive letters commenting on their work from people anxious to get into the act by supplying the author with more information. This happens especially with contemporary history and biography. Thus, authors gather unsolicited, additional material after publication that they wish they had acquired before their work went to press. If you correspond with the authors of books and articles that you are using in your research work, you may elicit fresh material, never in print, which came to the authors in this way. That is, if they are willing to share it.

Interviewing

Obtaining information by interview is an art in itself. Some people will always find it difficult because they do not have the kind of personality that invites interviewees to talk freely and frankly. To others with an outgoing nature that inspires confidence, even intimacy, interviewing comes easily and naturally. Whatever kind of person you may be, however, you can become a more effective interviewer by following certain basic rules.

Do your homework first

It is a waste of your time, and insulting to the interviewee, to ask questions which you could have answered yourself by advance preparation. Concentrate instead on filling gaps in the written record by asking people why they decided or did certain things. Or ask their opinions on subjects where they are not known. Let them respect you for having done your homework before you called on them for assistance.

Establish your relationship with the interviewee

You get the best results from interviews by letting your subjects know just who you are, and your purpose in interviewing them. Only then will they feel relaxed in answering questions and confident in telling you things they might not take the time to tell others. If at all possible, try to give them a reason why their co-operation in the interview will fulfil some interest of theirs, such as helping obtain recognition for a relative or an old friend for an important accomplishment – or even for themselves.

Let the interviewee talk

Ask your questions, then try to intrude as little as possible, except to direct your subject to the points on which you want information. It is better to let an interviewee ramble than for you, the interviewer, to do too much of the talking. The purpose of the interview, after all, is for you to draw information from whoever you are talking to, not the other way round.

Write down your interview record immediately

Whether you take shorthand notes during an interview, or write longhand, or use a recorder, it is important to write out the record of an interview as soon as possible. The reason is that no one's record is complete, and you can interpolate items that you remember. The act of transcribing the interview when it is fresh in your mind helps you to fill gaps and correct errors. It also reminds you of possible further questions, which you may be able to put to your subject at another meeting or by telephone.

When your transcript is complete it is often productive to give a copy to the interviewee, who may catch some errors, and may even enlarge on what you were told during the interview.

When tape recording an interview, ask permission

The tape recorder has become essential to some interviewers, who would feel lost without it. Others feel no need whatsoever for a recording device because they are adept at shorthand or speedy note-taking and see no need to record every word uttered by the interviewee. When you do wish to record an interview you should ask permission to do so, because some people, perhaps without good reason, are reluctant to have their words recorded. In fact, it would be unethical for a researcher to record an interview secretly.

When the interviewee has agreed to the use of a recording device, the interviewer should take the precaution to place it out of sight so that it is less distracting to the person being interviewed. Frequently someone who has been somewhat uncertain, even inhibited, at the start of a recorded interview will loosen up and speak quite freely once the initial nervousness has worn off. This is most likely to occur when the recorder is out of sight because, as the interview proceeds, the interviewee usually forgets all about it.

ADVANCED TECHNIQUES

This section deals with techniques that will very rarely be used by the majority of researchers. However, as was pointed out in the first section, there will be methods or information sources cited in this chapter that some readers will argue should be in the 'Basic Approaches' section. Due to the many different types of researchers and the breadth of research topics undertaken there are bound to be some approaches that are more or less relevant to each reader. Do not be put off by the title 'Advanced Techniques'. If the information you need when you are beginning your work is contained within this section, then now is the right time to read it!

Search Out the Trade Press

The specialized trade press is a rich source of detailed information for the researcher. For the most part it is commercial, being slanted toward news and advertising aimed to help people in the same economic activity, or specialists engaged in similar work, to perform more efficiently, to cut costs and thus to prosper economically. There is a press for virtually every interest group in the country – professionals, those in business, craftspeople or specialists in one line of work – whether they are organized or not. Closely allied to the trade press is the hobbyist's press, which the hobbyist does not read for economic gain, but which is definitely published for that purpose.

The trade press is frequently overlooked in research, or not given the attention it is worth, for several reasons. Among them is the fact that academics generally do not inform students that there is such a thing as the trade press, or dismiss it as unscholarly. In addition, because the readership of most trade periodicals is such a specialized group, general libraries can afford to carry only a small proportion of them, and indexes to periodicals cover only a small section of them. There are so many specialized trade journals, magazines and newsletters published in the UK, and so many new ones appear each year while others disappear by merger, that no lists can be completely up to date. But there are a number of ways to find the standard trade press sources for a given inquiry.

For *Directories*, many of which are annuals, the best source of information is *Current British Directories* (see p. 53). If your library has it, here is a sound first step in pursuing the trade press. The directories to which it leads often carry advertising for other reference sources, such as trade periodicals and newsletters.

For *Periodicals* there are three useful directories, in which the trade press is mingled alphabetically by subject field with non-commercial periodicals. *Willing's Press Guide* and *Benn's Media Directory*, UK volume (both described on p. 51), list British publications. *Benn's* also publish an international volume covering 195 countries. The third is *Ulrich's International Periodicals Directory*, which lists titles from other countries in all parts of the world.

Another way to start is to consult the specialized periodicals index (see p. 38) that in your judgement comes closest to your field of inquiry. By examining the list of periodical titles inside the front cover you can find a few titles of magazines and journals that cover your field in general, or come close to it. By examining copies of these (and for this you may have to visit a specialized library) you may find references to other publications in the field, and advertisements for them. Certainly the editors of periodicals of broader coverage know about the others of narrower scope with which they compete, or from which they draw information for their own use.

Still another starting-point is with companies, organizations and associations, through which you can find the specialists who would know their own trade press. The researcher can then go directly to the target by asking the specialized craftsperson, or professional, or person in business: 'What trade journals do you read?'; 'Which ones do your colleagues read?'; 'Which are your best printed sources of information?'; and, 'Do you have copies of them?' Ask specifically about magazines, journals, newsletters and directories. This personal approach is often more productive than trying to track down highly specialized trade publications in libraries, where most of them are not to be found. The total circulation of a specialized trade journal

may be very limited with perhaps only a handful of subscribers in your city. In this case the public library may
never have been asked to subscribe to a journal so specialized; and the librarians have not heard of it. Go instead to
the practitioners who need the trade press for their work,
and ask them.

The Librarians' Guide to Reference Books

The standard work in which librarians look up reference
book titles to suggest to readers is *Walford's Guide to
Reference Material*. Because *Walford's Guide* is a comprehensive work containing only brief descriptions of
books on all kinds of subjects, no librarian can be expected
to master its contents, nor to give a sound judgement of the
value of many of the books listed under a given subject.
But an experienced reference librarian can help you find
the headings and pages you want in it before turning it
over to you.

It is worth the time of every serious research worker to
inspect this source and to become generally familiar with
its contents and organization. When taking up a new
subject, the researcher can check *Walford's Guide* under
the headings relevant to the work and note the reference
books that may be useful. By inspecting these early in the
project, you may save time by finding that someone else
has already collected and put into print the material you
want.

Interlibrary Loan

If you need a particular book that is not available in a
library convenient to where you live you can obtain it
through Interlibrary Loan. Interlibrary Loan is a co-
operative system by which libraries in all parts of the

country lend books to one another on order for the use of readers who have requested them. The book can normally be used by the reader outside the borrowing library. However, in the case of unpublished theses they can be used only at the borrowing library.

Loans are granted to approved organizations using the printed requisition forms. In order to obtain a book through the Interlibrary Loan system you must fill in the form provided at your local public or university/polytechnic library. All you have to do is enter the title of the book, the name of the author and the publisher. The librarian will then check through the internal library network, in the South East, known as *LASER* (London and South East Region Interlibrary Loan), to ascertain where the book is situated. Books ordered through Interlibrary Loan take between one and two weeks to arrive. However, students who order unpublished theses should order them in plenty of time as some of the more obscure theses may have to be obtained from the university at which they were written. To this end the Interlibrary Loan system has a network of contacts in other countries including the Library of Congress in America. The book must be returned to the borrowing library within a limited time (normally three weeks), after which it is returned to the lending library.

The service is normally free to students if they order the book from their institution's library. A small fee (in the order of pence rather than pounds) is charged to the general public when they order books through their local library.

The co-ordinating body of the Interlibrary Loan system is the British Library Lending Division. This is a lending library covering all subject fields and providing a rapid loan and photocopy service to organizations. The Library holds in stock about four million volumes of books and periodicals, and over three million documents in microfilm, including:

- 55,000 different serial titles currently being received covering all subjects and in all languages

- 484,000 translations into English, mainly from Russian scientific and technical serials.

- 2,429,000 monographs.

- over 2,000,000 unclassified technical reports mainly of US origin

- 383,000 doctoral theses including doctoral theses from most British universities

- 68,000 music scores

- 166,000 conference proceedings; all British official publications from 1962, all UNESCO publications from 1954, and all EEC publications from 1973, with considerable stocks from previous years in these categories.

In addition to the lending service offered through Inter-library Loan, the British Library Documents Supply Centre also has a public reading room.

Finding Unpublished Doctoral Dissertations

For many years until the 1950s, the hundreds, even thousands, of unpublished doctoral dissertations, or theses, presented in British universities each year by candidates for Master's or doctoral degrees represented a huge research resource that was very difficult to tap. These papers were the fruit of tremendous work, particularly in the compilation of bibliographies and in manuscript research. Yet until recent years it was a challenge to all but the most specialized scholars to find out whether a dissertation had been written on a given subject, because the dissertations were not published. In most cases students had deposited a typescript of the dissertation at the university, and retained a copy themselves. Most researchers would never find their way to this work because it was not indexed anywhere as a published book.

Today, however, one can locate unpublished dissertations by consulting the *Index to Theses*, published by Aslib and carried in many research libraries. To give this index its full name, it is the *Index to Theses Accepted for Higher Degrees by the Universities of Great Britain and Ireland and the Council for National Academic Awards.* The index carries both a list of subject headings in fairly broad terms and a subject index extracting specific terms from titles, so as to assist a search into particular topics. It also carries a list of authors. A certain number of Master's degree theses are included. The *Index to Theses* is issued twice annually. There are no cumulations of the thirty-odd volumes that have appeared since the mid-1950s, so the researcher must consult one issue after another in pursuit of the subject.

Finding a reference to an unpublished dissertation in the index is the researcher's first step; obtaining the thesis itself is the second. In 1954 the Standing Conference of National and University Libraries (SCONUL) proposed a co-operative system whereby at least one copy of every thesis should be deposited in the university library, and authors would be asked to permit their thesis to be available for interlibrary loan and for photocopying. This scheme was put into operation, and then in 1971 the service it provided was expanded when universities were asked to provide copies of doctoral theses to the British Library Lending Division (BLLD) to be microfilmed, then returned. On request for a thesis held on microfilm, a duplicate is lent from this central source. If wished, the researcher can purchase a duplicate film or a paper copy.

Close to fifty British institutions of higher education have been co-operating in this scheme starting at various dates since the early 1970s, and more than 40,000 theses are now available from BLLD.

Digging into Manuscripts and Papers

There comes a time in many a research project when printed sources will no longer do, and you must look for information in original handwritten or typewritten documents. The most fruitful place to hunt for them is in research libraries. Historians usually call such documents 'original sources'; librarians use the term 'manuscripts'. Both historians and librarians also use the term 'papers' – under which they group letters, notes, diaries, business accounts, logbooks, reports, drafts, and so forth. In some cases papers may have been copied in longhand by clerks or duplicated (by letterpress or carbon copy) in very small numbers, but have not been generally distributed.

Research in manuscript collections is always a challenge, because you never know what you will find, or whether you will find what you want. In a sense a day spent examining papers in a manuscript collection is like a day's fishing: you do not know whether you will end the day with a good catch or go home empty-handed. But for excitement it far exceeds reading material in print because you have the sense of discovery, of being there first. In fact, this very excitement can lead you down fascinating paths away from your subject, and if you do not guard yourself against distractions you can lose sight of your original purpose in digging into the papers.

The first step in manuscript work is to find out whether there are any collections of papers likely to be helpful in your research, and if so, where they are. Useful manuscripts may be found in the hands of private individuals (see

p. 67), or in the files of organizations (p. 65), but for those that are held by libraries and other repositories, the following sources are of considerable value:

- The Department of Manuscripts at the British Museum is part of the British Library Reference Division. The researcher can find out what manuscripts are held in the Department by consulting *The Catalogues of the Manuscript Collections in the British Museum* edited by T. C. Skeat and published by the British Museum. Recent acquisitions are listed by number in a series of volumes held on the open shelves in the Student's Room of the Department of Manuscripts.

- To find where other collections of manuscripts and private papers are located you should contact the Royal Commission on Historical Manuscripts, which keeps a **National Register of Archives.**

Once you have located a certain collection of papers and have arrived at the library where they are deposited, it is always valuable to ask whether there is an index, guide or register (the terms vary) to assist you. Unless asked, a library assistant may fail to inform you that a typewritten guide to the contents of the papers is available. So you should routinely ask whether there is an index to the collection. In large collections using an index is a great time-saver, because papers relating to a given subject may be scattered through many years of a collection of letters that is organized chronologically. Or they may be grouped together because the person whose papers you are examining may have kept his or her files that way. There are mixed views among manuscript curators as to methods of organization of collections; consequently there is no uniformity. Frequently manuscript collections are left as they were when they were given to the repository – organized in part by subject, in part alphabetically by name of correspondent, and in part chronologically. It is up to researchers to find their way, and a register can save a great deal of needle-in-haystack hunting.

An important part of the technique of manuscript research lies in thinking carefully about which people, and which organizations, would have been concerned with the subject of your research. Then look for their papers.

A fine point, useful as a time-saver: ask the curator of manuscripts for the names of other people who have recently done research in the same collections. Then ask those people if they can and will save you time by pinpointing items or dates that you need. Unless they look on you as a direct competitor, other researchers are usually willing to co-operate in this way, knowing that you in turn may come across items that are helpful to them. Thus two scholars can be of mutual assistance.

Publishing an Author's Query

In certain kinds of research, especially in biography or survey research, it can be useful to make public your need for information, in the hope that volunteers will make contact with you. This is best done by publishing an author's query in several newspapers or scholarly journals best calculated to get results. An author's query can profitably be placed in the letters column of the major national dailies or local newspapers.

As a 'querying author' (researcher), you take your chances on being overwhelmed with familiar material that you neither need nor want. Your best protection is to phrase the query so that its scope is plainly limited. It can specify that the writer is seeking 'those with personal knowledge' of the subject or 'original letters and manuscripts'. Even if no worthwhile information results from the published query, the time taken to publish it is minimal. But it may open entirely new avenues of research, particularly through interview, and lead directly to fresh sources of written material.

Obtaining Out-of-Print Books

There are situations in research work when you want to obtain your own copy of an out-of-print book, one that you can no longer buy from an ordinary retail bookshop or direct from the publisher. This occurs when you need a book for reference over a long period, and it is inconvenient to consult a library copy on every occasion.

Book-search specialists

The best method to get your own copy is to use the services offered by a book-search specialist in the out-of-print book market. Some are connected with bookshops; others work from their homes with no stock on hand. The expert book-finder is a vanishing species, but as long as some of them are around they will perform a service at reasonable cost that no amateur can hope to match. Their classified 'ads' can be found in literary journals and in *The Times Literary Supplement*. These specialists use an inexpensive communication network among their colleagues (including printed lists of books wanted), by which they can reach all the known out-of-print book dealers by mail or telephone. Your inquiry for a given title thus becomes known to a large circle of dealers. Those who can supply the book communicate with your dealer, who in turn notifies you. Reputable dealers rate the physical condition of each book as 'excellent', 'good', 'fair', etc., and charge accordingly.

Out-of-print bookshops

Researchers who live in cities big enough to support one or

more out-of-print or secondhand and antiquarian book-shops can go to the shop and spend time looking for what they want on the shelves. They can also leave a book-search request with the shop, provided it offers a book-search service. Prices of books which you locate in a shop are likely to be lower than those obtained through the network of out-of-print dealers, so it sometimes saves money to hunt in a few shops yourself and save the service mark-up. To find out the names and addresses of out-of-print bookshops in your locality consult **Cole's Register of British Antiquarian and Secondhand Bookdealers**, published by The Clique Ltd.

University Microfilms International (UMI)

A relatively new method of obtaining a copy of an out-of-print book is to have a copy (or copies) made to order. This service is offered by UMI (see also p. 88) through its **Books On Demand** programme (for information call 0883 844123). When it receives an inquiry for a xerographic or microfilm copy of a particular book, UMI first looks into its catalogue of nearly 100,000 book titles already on film in its vault to see if that title is on hand. If so, the customer is quoted a price, which is based largely on the size of the book. If necessary, UMI can also draw on tens of thousands of other titles available through other divisions of the company, and through co-operating publishers who will lend UMI a rare book so that a negative can be made. The charge in this case is higher than for a book already on film.

Reprints

Watch for the long out-of-print title to reappear in a reprint edition. With the recent development of efficient, inexpensive photo-reproduction methods, which can replace costly typesetting, it has become economic for publishers to issue reprint editions. The reprint book industry has burgeoned since 1960, to the point where there are hundreds of reprint book publishers active in the United Kingdom. Many are specialists in subjects that have attracted great interest recently – such as black biography. Some are able to publish hard cover reprint editions profitably in quantities as low as 300–400, about 20 per cent of the number of copies required for profitability in normal publishing with its high typesetting costs. Tens of thousands of titles, once out of print, are now available from reprint publishers.

Oral History Collections

A new kind of research resource has appeared since 1948 – the oral history collection. An oral history collection consists of tapes and typed transcripts of interviews recorded by trained interviewers with people having memories of important events or personalities. These interviews have added substantially to the written documentation of the recent past because they have tapped the knowledge of people who for one reason or another could not, or would not, take the time to write them down. One hour of skilled interviewing can result in a document of great research value that otherwise might never have been produced. This is particularly the case with information obtained from old people, and from extremely busy people who are not used to writing. Oral history collections are most frequently projects of universities, libraries and historical societies. They concentrate on the memories and comments of prominent people, or on those with intimate knowledge of the prominent. There are special purpose collections, however, concentrating on the history of a locality, a company, an industry, or even an entire movement.

Researchers who need access to oral information would

be well advised to seek out *Oral History*, the journal of the Oral History Society. The Society's *Directory of British Oral Collections* lists entries in alphabetical order but also has subject and place indexes. For oral collections in other countries consult the American publication *Oral History Collections*.

Specialized Sources of Information

There are so many specialized sources of information available to the thorough research worker that it would be futile to attempt to list them all. There is no substitute for remaining constantly alert to the possibility of fresh sources of which you may not yet have heard, but which are a familiar story to others. In addition, new information services are coming into being all the time, as man's need to know in detail becomes more pressing, and as the technology for recording, storing, retrieving, transmitting and duplicating information moves rapidly forward. Here are a few specialized sources among many:

Treasury and Cabinet Office Library
The library holds copies of all Parliamentary documents as well as all documents issued by the Central Statistical Office (CSO). The library is open to the public but you must arrange an appointment first (telephone 071-270-5290). The CSO also has an information service for the public. If you want to know whether statistics on certain subjects are available you can telephone 071-270-6363 or 071-270-6364 and ask. However, it is courteous to do as much preliminary research as you can and to phone for assistance only when you have exhausted your own sources of information.

United Nations Publications
Since its foundation the United Nations has published and

placed on sale an increasing amount of documentation on a wide variety of subjects of public and international concern. UN material is produced in clothbound and paperbound books, pamphlets, periodicals and official records, both printed and in multilith form. Much of it is recurrent – in yearbooks or annual surveys, bulletins, series and annual reports. All are published in English, and in many cases they are available in French, Spanish and Russian.

Subject categories of UN publications include, among others: cartography, economics, social questions, international law, transport and communications, atomic energy, narcotic drugs, demography, human rights, public finance, international statistics and treaties. The publications of the intergovernmental agencies (commonly considered as related to the UN) are available through their own separate sales organizations, addresses of which can be obtained from the UN Information Centre Library, Ship House, 20 Buckingham Gate, London SW1 (tel: 071-630-1981). Some of these intergovernmental agencies are: the International Labour Organization; Food and Agriculture Organization; World Health Organization; International Monetary Fund; Universal Postal Union.

University Microfilms International (UMI)

Because of the speed and thoroughness with which it is putting new technology to use in forms of interest to the researcher, this subsidiary of the Xerox Corporation warrants separate consideration as an information source. UMI offers such a variety of services in the microfilm and reprint fields that it is worth while for the serious investigator to obtain its full line of catalogues to see whether it has recently added a service that was not offered last year. UMI can be contacted at White Swan House, Godstone, Surrey, RH9 8LW (tel: 0883-844123). (See also p. 85.)

Library Classification Systems Can Help You

If you learn something about the way libraries classify their books, and if you gain access to the stacks, you will find the books you need more quickly and easily. Whatever system your reference library may use you should learn at the outset what system it employs. Second, you should ask for whatever printed guide or list is at hand that is used by the libraries to classify their newly acquired books. Such a list can steer you to books on the subjects you want to cover.

The most commonly used classification system in libraries in Britain is the **Dewey Decimal Classification**. This Classification system uses ten major categories, which are in turn sub-divided to allow for finer classification of related subjects. The major categories are, General Works (000), Philosophy (100) Religion (200), Social Science (300), Languages (400), Science (500), Technology (600), Art and Recreations (700), Literature (800) and Geography, Biography and History (900).

Services from Periodicals

Periodicals, especially magazines with a long history of excellence in their specialities, sometimes provide services to the researcher that cannot be obtained elsewhere. Whether a given periodical will help you depends on the seriousness with which the staff takes your query, and the time and resources available. Frequently an inquiry from a subscriber or a 'constant reader' will elicit an attempt to be helpful, because this is considered to be part of the magazine's public relations effort.

Back issues, as long as they last, are frequently supplied for nominal prices to those who write for them. Offprints of specified articles or pages, or photocopies of them, are often supplied free. Scientific journals print extra copies of articles routinely to supply to those who write to the journal requesting them, and frequently the author of the article, who is not on the staff of the periodical, will have a supply of offprints for distribution on request.

Another service, requiring more time of the magazine staff, is a search of the office index of the periodical in order to respond to a specific query. For instance, the magazine might be asked for references in back issues in more detail than the researcher could get from the relevant published index. The chances are excellent that the magazine maintains its own cumulated office index in fine detail. Many magazines and periodicals produce an annual index which can be found with the bound volumes in the library.

Beyond the Written Word: Multimedia Sources

The last few years have seen a rapid expansion in the production and use of films, filmstrips, slides, tapes and transparencies as means of communication and instruction. To a great extent they have been produced as educational materials, the primary sales target being schools and other educational establishments. They have also been produced as training aids for organizations in business and for government-related agencies, such as the military, and they have been produced and circulated for public relations and sales purposes. In addition, tapes of programmes originating from radio and television stations are at times available for rental or sale. All of these non-print forms of communication can have value for the individual doing research, because one can often learn from them things that print cannot convey.

There are two useful sources of film and audio material that the researcher should contact.

- **National Firm Archive** holds film material as well as other material dealing with the history of the film industry. The National Film Archive is based in London (tel: 071-437-4355)

- **The British Library National Sound Archive** holds vast amounts of recorded material which can be accessed by the general public on request. The Archive has an excellent information service and will help researchers to find the recorded material they require. The Archive is also based in London and can be contacted on 071-589-6603.

One should not overlook the possibility that special libraries, and the headquarters of associations, have all kinds of non-print materials that they have collected on a casual basis. A company library or its public relations office, for example, may not have intended to make a collection, but it may have become the repository for such things as a tape recording of the remarks made at the retirement dinner for an outgoing president; informal photographs of company events intended for a newsletter; or home movies made by a company officer showing colleagues at play, and turned over to the company by his or her survivors. It is therefore worth while to ask about such informally collected items that might not normally be listed in a library's catalogue of holdings.

Keeping Alert to New Technology

Since the mid-1960s, new information technology has been developed and put to use at an increasingly rapid rate. For instance, there has been miniaturization, first in the form of microfilm reels; then on microfiche which are 4 in. × 6 in. film cards reproducing about sixty standard pages; and more recently an ultramicrofiche, which can hold up to 3,000 pages on one 4 in. × 6 in. film card (thirty-five rows of tiny pictures, each with eighty-five pages). There are combination viewer-printers which enlarge a filmed page for viewing on a screen, and can then produce a paper copy of the page being shown. There are distance-duplicating systems by which a paper copy can be produced in one city from an original placed into the duplicating-transmission equipment in another city. There are thousands of computer-based banks of data, such as company personnel records, the details of which are known only to the few people responsible for using them. There are computerized information systems that print out, on command, all kinds of information ranging from short bibliographies to lengthy series of article abstracts.

Many reference librarians and university scholars whose degrees were obtained before such innovations are not fully aware of some of the new fact-finding methods this technology has made possible. They therefore cannot always guide students and other researchers in their use. Nor is there a foolproof method for keeping abreast of all new research resources. The best we can do is to remain constantly alert to the fact that new resources are appearing all the time. We should not hesitate to ask at companies, libraries, public agencies, publishers, etc. what new services they may have added lately, and what they know about what neighbouring organizations have added.

The on-line computer search systems available through the local or academic library can be a fast, efficient way of finding out what has been written about a particular subject. The best way of finding out what computerized search services are available to the researcher is to go to a library and ask the librarian to explain what systems they operate and which ones are most appropriate to the subject being pursued.

These are time-saving devices that can produce a huge collection of references very quickly, but they all rest on the research and indexing skill of the people behind the scenes who compiled the references in the first place, following the research principles outlined in this book. If the human being who did the original research overlooked a few references, the electronic machine will not produce them.

For the researcher the art of using computer-based information systems lies first in finding out what data organizations have stored in their computers that can be used; and second, in getting permission, or authority, to retrieve the data, if any is there. Of course, there have for some years been organizations which have compiled specialized information in computers, particularly in the natural sciences, and have supplied customers with printouts according to their specifications. A pharmaceutical manufacturer, for example, might request a list of all scientific journal articles containing the words 'heart' or 'blood' in the title, and such a list is easily produced.

A critical point for the computer as a research instrument, just as in the standard written indexes of books and periodicals, is in the accuracy of the indexer. An error at the coding stage can, in fact, be even more damaging in a computer than in traditional written form, because the error on magnetic tape is more difficult to detect. Therefore, research workers should look on the computer as a time-saving electronic file, but not as a 'brain' or as an instrument that will replace their own powers to observe and to think.

References

Accounting and Data Processing Abstracts, Anbar Abstracting Services, published in association with The Institute of Chartered Accountants in England and Wales

Antiques and Collector's Index, Clover Publications, Bedfordshire (quarterly).

Benn's Media Directory, Benn's Business Information Services Ltd, Kent (yearly)

Biography Index, H. W. Wilson Co., New York (quarterly)

Bookseller, J. Whitaker & Sons Ltd, London (weekly)

British Books in Print, J. Whitaker & Sons Ltd, London (yearly)

British Education Index, University of Leeds, Brotherton Library, Leeds (quarterly)

British Humanities Index, Library Association, London (quarterly)

Business Pages, British Telecommunications PLC (annual)

Chronological and Occupational Index to the Dictionary of National Biography, Oxford University Press, Oxford

Clover Information Index, Clover Publications, Bedfordshire (quarterly)

Cole's Register of British Antiquarian and Secondhand Bookdealers 1989, The Clique Ltd, York (yearly)

Concise Dictionary of National Biography, Oxford University Press, Oxford

Current Biography, H. W. Wilson Co., New York (yearly)

Current Biography Cumulated Index, H. W. Wilson Co., New York (latest edition 1986)

Current British Directories, CBD Research Ltd, Kent (latest edition 1988)

Current European Directories, CBD Research Ltd, Kent, 1981

Current Index to Journals in Education, Oryx Press, Phoenix, Arizona (monthly)

Current Law, Sweet & Maxwell Ltd, London

Current Law Index, Information Access Company, California (monthly)

Current Technology Index, Library Association Publishing Ltd, London (monthly)

Dictionary of American Biography, American Council of Learned Societies

Dictionary of National Biography, Oxford University Press, Oxford (updated every decade)

Directory of British Associations and Associations in Ireland, Henderson, G. P. and Henderson, S. P. A. (Eds), CBD Research Ltd, Kent (latest edition 1990)

Directory of British Oral History Collections, Oral History Society, 1981

Directory of European Associations, CBD Research Ltd, Kent, 1986

Dod's Parliamentary Companion, Dod's Parliamentary Companion Ltd, Herstmonceux, E. Sussex (annual)

Education Yearbook, Longman Group Ltd.

Encyclopaedia Britannica, Chicago, London, 32 vols (latest edition 1989)

Guardian, printed in London and Manchester (daily)

Guide to Reference Material, Library Association, London

Hansard's Parliamentary Debates: House of Commons and House of Lords, HMSO

Hollis Press and Public Relations Annual, Hollis Directories, Sunbury-on-Thames, Middx, 1989

Index to Legal Periodicals, H. W. Wilson Co., New York

Index to The Times, Times Newspapers, London and Manchester (monthly)

Index to Theses Accepted for Higher Degrees by the Universities of Great Britain and Ireland and the Council for National Academic Awards, ASLIB, London (twice yearly)

International Books in Print, Bowker, New York, 1989

International Who's Who, 1989–90, Europa Publications Limited,London (53rd edition)

International Yearbook and Statesman's Who's Who, Macmillan, London, 1988

Marketing and Distribution Abstracts, Anbar Management Publications

New York Times Obituaries Index, Microfilming Corp. (1858–1968) 1970, (1969–1978) 1980

O'Dwyer's Directory of Corporate Communications, New York

O'Dwyer's Directory of Public Relations Firms, New York

Pears Cyclopaedia, Pelham Books, London (yearly)

Personnel and Training Abstracts, Anbar Management Publications

Popular Medical Index, Mede Publishing (quarterly)

Readers' Guide to Periodical Literature, Wilson, New York

Research Index – Finance, Business Surveys Ltd (fortnightly)

RILA – (Répertoire International de la Littérature de l'Art), Bibliographic service of the J. Paul Getty Trust (semi-annually)

Sectional Lists, HMSO

The Times, Times Newspapers, Manchester and London

The Times Index, Reading Research Publications

Top Management Abstracts, Anbar Management Publications

Trade Associations and Professional Bodies in the United

Kingdom, 10th edition, Gale Research International, Andover, Kent

Ulrich's International Periodicals Directory: a Classified Guide to Current Periodicals, Foreign and Domestic, 1989 edition, Bowker, London, New York

Walford's Guide to Reference Material, Walford, A. J. (Ed) London, Library Association

Whitaker's Almanack, 1990, J. Whitaker & Sons Ltd, London, (122nd edition)

Who Was Who (7 volumes to 1980), A. & C. Black, London

Who's Who 1990, A. & C. Black, London, (142nd annual edition)

Who's Who in America (44th revised edition), Marquis, Chicago, 1986

Willing's Press Guide: A Comprehensive Index and Handbook of the Press of the United Kingdom and Great Britain, Thomas Skinner Directories, East Grinstead (yearly)

Index

A C Black, London, 48
A Low-Cost Home Reference
    Collection, 32
Access to Library Stacks, 45
*Accounting and Data Processing
    Abstracts*, 52
Alumni Offices, 64
*Anbar Abstracting Services –
    Business Management*, 52
Anbar Management Publications,
    52
Antiques and Collector's Index, 26
*Aslib Directory of Information
    Sources in the United Kingdom*,
    18, 20
Associations, 65

Benn's Media Directory, 51, 62, 76
Best Guide to Reference Books, 21
Bibliographical notes, 40
Biographical directories, 38
Biographical Reference: A Few
    Useful Books, 49
Biography Index, 50
Bodleian Library, 45
'Bookfinders', 84
'Books On Demand', 85
Bookseller, The, 32
British Books in Print, 31, 32, 37
British Education Index, 26
British Humanities Index, 24, 25,
    38
British Library, The, 45
British Library Department of
    Manuscripts, 82

British Library Lending Division,
    78
British Library National Sound
    Archive, 91
British Medical Journal, 29
British Pages, 63, 65

Cambridge University Library, 45
Card Catalogues in Reference
    Libraries, 37
Catalogues of the Manuscript
    Collections in the British
    Library, 82
*Chronological and Occupational
    Index to the DNB*, 51
Citizens Advice Bureau (CAB),
    60
Clover Information Index, 27
*Cole's Register of British
    Antiquarian & Secondhand
    Bookdealers*, 85
Colindale Library, 48
Collections of manuscripts, 82
Columbia Encyclopaedia, 37
Compiling bibliographies, 8
Computerised databases, 14
*Concise Dictionary of National
    Biography*, 50
Conducting literature searches, 8
Copyright libraries, 45
Current Biography, 36
*Current Biography Cumulated
    Index*, 36
Current British Directories, 53, 75
Current European Directories, 54

Current Index to Journals in Education, 27
Current Law, 28
Current Law Index, 28
Current Technology Index, 27

Dewey Decimal Classification, 89
DIALOG Information Retrieval Service, 30
Dictionary of American Biography, 51
Dictionary of National Biography, 35, 50
Directory of British Associations and Associations in Ireland, 54, 63, 65, 68
Directory of British Directories, 53
Directory of British Oral Collections, 87
Directory of European Associations, 55
Doctoral dissertations, 79
Dod's Parliamentary Companion, 56

Education Yearbook, 22
Encyclopaedia Britannica, 36

Filing Business Cards, 69
Finding Periodicals on Particular Subjects, 51
Finding Reference Books in Libraries, 22
Finding Special Libraries in Your City, 19
Finding the Person Who Knows, 68
Finding the Right Library, 17

General Practitioner, 29
Good Housekeeping, 29
Government as an Information Source, 55
Guardian, The 25
Guide to Reference Materials, Walford's, 47, 77

Hansard, 56
Her Majesty's Stationery Office, 57, 58
Hollis Press and Public Relations Annual, 43

Index to Legal Periodicals, 28
Index to The Times, 23
Index to Theses Accepted for Higher Degrees by the Universities of Great Britain and Ireland and the CNAA, 80
Indexes to Newspapers Other than The Times, 48
Interlibrary Loan, 77
International Books in Print, 32
International Who's Who, 35
International Yearbook and Statesman's Who's Who, 35

Lancet, The, 29
Library Association, The, 18, 24, 47
Library of Congress, The, 78
Library's own catalogue, 22
Local Councils and Local Councillors, 63
London Library, 47

Magazines and journals, 13
Manuscripts, 13, 81
Marketing and Distribution Abstracts, 52
'MPs' Political & Social Interests', 56

National Association of Citizens Advice Bureaux (NACAB), 60
National Film Archive, 91
National Library of Scotland, 45
National Library of Wales, 45
National Register of Archives, 82
Newspaper indexes, 23, 48
Newspaper Reporters and Editors, 61

New York Times Index, 23, 37, 38
New York Times Obituaries Index, 37
Nursing Times, 29

Obituaries, 37
Observer, The, 25
Oral History, 87
Oral History Collections, 87
Oral History Society, 87
Organizations, 65
Organizations and Interest Groups, 68
Out-of-print bookshops, 84
O'Dwyer's Directory of Corporate Communications, 44
O'Dwyer's Directory of Public Relations Firms, 43

Palmer's Index to the Times, 23
Paperbacks in Print, 32
Pears Cyclopaedia, 33
Periodical Indexes, 38
Personal Files, 67
Personnel and Training Abstracts, 53
Popular Medical Index, 29
Printed Reference Materials, 47
Public and University Libraries, 66
Public Relations Sources, 42, 62

RAA (Repertoire d'Art et d'Archaeologie), 30
Readers' Guide to Periodical Literature, 25, 38
Reference libraries, 45
Research Index – Finance, 29
RILA – the International Art Index, 30
Royal Commission on Historical Manuscripts, 82

Sectional Lists, HMSO, 59
Special duplicated documents, 13
Special Libraries, 19, 66

Specialized News Reporters and Editors, 69
Standing Conference of National and University Libraries, 80
Subject Index to Periodicals, 25
Sunday Times, 23, 25

Thompson Local Directory, 64, 65
Times Index, The, 37, 38
Times, The, 25
Times Educational Supplement, 23
Times Higher Education Supplement, 23
Times Literary Supplement, 23, 84
Top Management Abstracts, 53
Trade Associations, 62
Trade Associations and Professional Bodies in the UK, 63
Trade press, 75
Treasury and Cabinet Office Library, 87
Trinity College Library, 45

Ulrich's International Periodicals Directory, 76
United Nations Publications, 87
University Microfilms International, 85, 88
Unpublished theses and dissertations, 13

Vacher's Parliamentary Companion, 34

Walford's Guide to Reference Material, 21, 77
Whitaker's Almanack, 33, 63
Who Was Who, 35
Who's Who, 34, 35
Who's Who in America, 35
Who's Who in International Organisations, 35
Who's Who in the World, 35
Willing's Press Guide, 51, 62, 76
Woman's Own, 29
Work Study & O & M Abstracts, 53

FOR THE BEST IN PAPERBACKS, LOOK FOR THE

In every corner of the world, on every subject under the sun, Penguin represents quality and variety – the very best in publishing today.

For complete information about books available from Penguin – including Puffins, Penguin Classics and Arkana – and how to order them, write to us at the appropriate address below. Please note that for copyright reasons the selection of books varies from country to country.

In the United Kingdom: Please write to *Dept E.P., Penguin Books Ltd, Harmondsworth, Middlesex, UB7 0DA.*

If you have any difficulty in obtaining a title, please send your order with the correct money, plus ten per cent for postage and packaging, to *PO Box No 11, West Drayton, Middlesex*

In the United States: Please write to *Dept BA, Penguin, 299 Murray Hill Parkway, East Rutherford, New Jersey 07073*

In Canada: Please write to *Penguin Books Canada Ltd, 2801 John Street, Markham, Ontario L3R 1B4*

In Australia: Please write to the *Marketing Department, Penguin Books Australia Ltd, P.O. Box 257, Ringwood, Victoria 3134*

In New Zealand: Please write to the *Marketing Department, Penguin Books (NZ) Ltd, Private Bag, Takapuna, Auckland 9*

In India: Please write to *Penguin Overseas Ltd, 706 Eros Apartments, 56 Nehru Place, New Delhi, 110019*

In the Netherlands: Please write to *Penguin Books Netherlands B.V., Postbus 195, NL–1380AD Weesp*

In West Germany: Please write to *Penguin Books Ltd, Friedrichstrasse 10–12, D–6000 Frankfurt/Main 1*

In Spain: Please write to *Longman Penguin España, Calle San Nicolas 15, E–28013 Madrid*

In Italy: Please write to *Penguin Italia s.r.l., Via Como 4, I-20096 Pioltello (Milano)*

In France: Please write to *Penguin Books Ltd, 39 Rue de Montmorency, F-75003 Paris*

In Japan: Please write to *Longman Penguin Japan Co Ltd, Yamaguchi Building, 2–12–9 Kanda Jimbocho, Chiyoda-Ku, Tokyo 101*

FOR THE BEST IN PAPERBACKS, LOOK FOR THE

PENGUIN REFERENCE BOOKS

The New Penguin English Dictionary

Over 1,000 pages long and with over 68,000 definitions, this cheap, compact and totally up-to-date book is ideal for today's needs. It includes many technical and colloquial terms, guides to pronunciation and common abbreviations.

The Penguin Spelling Dictionary

What are the plurals of *octopus* and *rhinoceros*? What is the difference between *stationary* and *stationery*? And how about *annex* and *annexe*, *agape* and *Agape*? This comprehensive new book, the fullest spelling dictionary now available, provides the answers.

Roget's Thesaurus of English Words and Phrases   Betty Kirkpatrick (ed.)

This new edition of Roget's classic work, now brought up to date for the nineties, will increase anyone's command of the English language. Fully cross-referenced, it includes synonyms of every kind (formal or colloquial, idiomatic and figurative) for almost 900 headings. It is a must for writers and utterly fascinating for any English speaker.

The Penguin Dictionary of Quotations

A treasure-trove of over 12,000 new gems and old favourites, from Aesop and Matthew Arnold to Xenophon and Zola.

The Penguin Wordmaster Dictionary
Martin H. Manser and Nigel D. Turton

This dictionary puts the pleasure back into word-seeking. Every time you look at a page you get a bonus – a panel telling you everything about a particular word or expression. It is, therefore, a dictionary to be read as well as used for its concise and up-to-date definitions.

FOR THE BEST IN PAPERBACKS, LOOK FOR THE 🐧

PENGUIN REFERENCE BOOKS

The Penguin Guide to the Law

This acclaimed reference book is designed for everyday use and forms the most comprehensive handbook ever published on the law as it affects the individual.

The Penguin Medical Encyclopedia

Covers the body and mind in sickness and in health, including drugs, surgery, medical history, medical vocabulary and many other aspects. 'Highly commendable' – *Journal of the Institute of Health Education*

The Slang Thesaurus

Do you make the public bar sound like a gentleman's club? Do you need help in understanding *Minder*? The miraculous *Slang Thesaurus* will liven up your language in no time. You won't Adam and Eve it! A mine of funny, witty, acid and vulgar synonyms for the words you use every day.

The Penguin Dictionary of Troublesome Words   Bill Bryson

Why should you avoid discussing the *weather conditions*? Can a married woman be *celibate*? Why is it eccentric to talk about the *aroma* of a cowshed? A straightforward guide to the pitfalls and hotly disputed issues in standard written English.

A Dictionary of Literary Terms

Defines over 2,000 literary terms (including lesser known, foreign language and technical terms), explained with illustrations from literature past and present.

The Concise Cambridge Italian Dictionary

Compiled by Barbara Reynolds, this work is notable for the range of examples provided to illustrate the exact meaning of Italian words and phrases. It also contains a pronunciation guide and a reference grammar.